THE FOURTH TRANSFORMATION

How Augmented Reality and Artificial Intelligence Change Everything

ROBERT SCOBLE & SHEL ISRAEL

Foreword by Gary Vaynerchuk

PATRICK BREWSTER PRESS
The Fourth Transformation:
How Augmented Reality & Artificial Intelligence Will Change Everything
Robert Scoble and Shel Israel

Editor: Josh Bernoff
Cover Design: Nico Nicomedes
Interior Design: Shawn Welch

Published in the United States by Patrick Brewster Press
ISBN-13: 978-1-5398-9444-5
ISBN-10: 1-5398944-4-4

1st Edition
Printed by CreateSpace, a DBA of On-Demand Publishing, LLC

Dedication

To Maryam & Paula for enduring us. To the kids and grandkids for carrying it forward.

About the Authors

Robert Scoble and Shel Israel have been researching, writing and speaking about technology's impact on the near-term future together and separately since 2005. They are best known for two critically acclaimed, best-selling tech business books: *Naked Conversations (2006)*, which demonstrated the business opportunities for social media, and *Age of Context (2012)*, which explained how the convergence of mobile, social media, IoT, data and location technologies would forever change the relationships between businesses and their customers.

Robert Scoble is entrepreneur in residence at *UploadVR* and among the world's best-known online tech journalists. He is recognized globally as an early spotter of important technology patterns and trends and is among the world's most popular tech speakers.

Shel Israel has written six previous books and has contributed to *Forbes*, *Fast Company* and *Businessweek*. He has been a keynote speaker at business and tech conferences on all continents not covered by ice.

Together, Scoble and Israel will continue to work together helping businesses find their way into and through the Fourth Transformation now starting.

+++++

Thanks to Our Sponsors

Telstra is Australia's leading telecommunications and technology company, offering a full range of communications services and competing in all telecommunications markets. In the 21st Century, opportunity belongs to connected businesses, governments, communities and individuals. As Australia's leading telecommunications and information services company, Telstra is proud to be helping our customers improve the ways in which they live and work through connection.

Aisle411 is an indoor mapping, location and analytics software solutions provider for the retail marketplace. Aisle411 delivers digital solutions through mobile devices, sensors, augmented reality and cloud-based systems to some of the world's largest brands with physical stores and venues.

OpenSesame, provides on-demand e-learning courses for the enterprise. Serving Global 2000 companies, OpenSesame delivers a flexible buying options to maximize learning budgets. Our broad catalog with 20,000+ courses from the world's leading publishers is updated constantly and is compatible with every LMS.

Additional thanks to Bram Cool as an individual contributor.

"Any sufficiently advanced technology
is indistinguishable from magic."

Arthur C. Clarke

Contents

Foreword: No Nevers

When I give speeches, I often ask, "Do you remember when you said 'never'?" When you said you'd never blog, never use Facebook, or never use Snapchat?

Well, now the new *never* is, "I'll never use augmented reality glasses," or "I'll never use virtual reality."

I've built my business and reputation on never listening to the "nevers." As you may know, I grew my family's wine store into a $60 million business and later built a digital agency with hundreds of employees, servicing some of the largest brands in the world—in part by jumping into new technologies that the market was undervaluing or simply not paying attention to.

The next waves of nevers are starting to emerge: virtual reality (VR) and augmented reality (AR)—and their cousin, mixed reality (MR).

In this book, my friends Robert Scoble and Shel Israel take you into how these nevers might affect your business. And let's get to the point: As of this writing, September 2016, you might already have a lot of opinions about this new virtual and wearable technology, including thinking it is too bulky, ugly, and dorky, while also being too expensive and not doing enough for you to be interested in using it.

But if you take the same approach that most of my audience did with social media (i.e., try to ignore the new form of communication and technology), you might not only miss huge learnings and opportunities to see how customers are shifting their behavior, but it might just put you out of business.

Why?

MR glasses are on their way to changing literally every part of human life. Pokemon Go was a huge wake up call. That's just an early taste of how augmented reality will change human life forever. It got people out in the streets looking for virtual characters.

And mixed reality will only add to this shift, as you'll be wearing glasses that will show you all sorts of amazing things layered on top of your everyday life. Already some of the tech in the market lets you work on virtual monitors, play with virtual holograms, and even entertain yourself with new kinds of volumetric entertainment.

True, I'm not yet wearing mixed reality glasses around town, but you won't find me saying "never," so much as "some day soon." I've built my businesses by being early on social networks and platforms. I already see the potential value these new technologies will bring over the next decade. I'll be watching closely, and, if this tech is as big as Scoble and Israel are predicting, then you can bet I'll jump in big time.

Anyone who hasn't paid attention to Mark Zuckerberg spending billions to acquire Oculus Rift or Apple's many purchases of augmented reality-focused companies is doing themselves a disservice. If you're in a position to get your hands on a VR headset, then you should, if only to get a taste for its current applications and its possible future implications. This technology is likely to change the media industry as we know it, including news, sports, movies, music, gaming and adult entertainment.

Outside of the gaming and entertainment components of VR/AR, what's even more telling is how corporations are utilizing its capabilities. Caterpillar is using augmented reality to train workers on how to properly maintain its tractors. Ford is using VR to design cars. Sephora has virtual lipstick and eyeliner that you try on your own face using your mobile phone. These are just some of the vast number of examples covered in this book.

Just talk to any of your friends who are on Snapchat about how fun its AR tech is. Not only can you barf rainbows with your friends, but the technology has also become a cool and lucrative opportunity for marketers.

You can surely bet that new smart glasses will drastically change how we watch TV. You're going to have many virtual screens around you in which you'll be able to watch your favorite sports teams, TV shows, or online videos while waiting in an airport lounge—even if there are no physical screens near you.

Imagine going to a New York Jets game, or any sporting event, while wearing these glasses. You'll be able to see a new level of player stats—anything from heart rates and blood oxygen levels to the intensity of the hits—displayed on top of the players on the field.

The NFL is putting sensors into footballs being used on the field. Someday you'll even be able to experience what it's like to be in the stadium and watch the game from my seat—all virtually. Where do you think this is all going? My friends Scoble and Israel will tell you it's a new MR media world.

That all sounds fun, right? But what about when you can use those glasses to order and deliver your meals? The implications are massive, and there's no question there will be a ton of new businesses opening up as the market evolves. I want to be there first, and so should you.

Pokemon Go taught us two lessons which will continue to be driven home over the next five years:

1. Mixing nostalgic brands everyone loves with new technology causes radically rapid adoption.
2. The tech industry now has platforms that will get people to buy and use new technologies in less than a week.

That's a radical change in expectations. Our world has sped up. Many local businesses saw increases in sales because they put signs out inviting players in. That's my kind of hustle.

Literally no part of your business will be untouched by this wave of new technology. That, my friends, opens up new opportunities for entrepreneurs like me, who ignore the naysayers and look to aggressively test and use this technology early—just as I used email, YouTube, blogging, Twitter, and Snapchat—to grow brands and businesses.

Because you have opened this book, it is obvious you are at least curious about what these new technologies are all about and to find out just what the hell a Fourth Transformation is. They tell you that on the next page.

Last but not least, a big congrats to my pals Robert and Shel for putting this story together in a style that any business person can understand, giving us all a preview into what will happen in the decades to come.

And one more thing: look forward to doing many more things you thought you would "never" do.

Gary Vaynerchuk, Founder & CEO, VaynerMedia

Introduction:
What's to Transform?

"A computer lets you make more mistakes faster than any invention in human history—with the possible exceptions of handguns and Tequila."

—Mitch Ratcliffe, digital thinker

I N THE BEGINNING, there were mainframes. They communicated only with a small, well-educated group of scientists and engineers who fed them punched cards.

Then stuff started happening.

At first we called them *paradigm shifts*, but then the marketers got hold of the term and worked it to death, so for this book, we'll call them *transformations* and make mainframes the starting point.

There have been three so far. The first came in the 1970s when people started using text characters to talk directly with computers. This transformation culminated when IBM licensed the MS-DOS operating system from Microsoft. It enabled many more people to use computers in more personal ways. Computing moved from clean rooms to desktops and beyond tech professionals to knowledge workers.

Then along came GUI. Apple introduced the Macintosh in 1984, which was followed a few years later with Microsoft Windows. The GUI was an essential stepping stone into the Worldwide Web, which greatly expanded what we could do with personal devices.

The third transformation came in 2007 with the iPhone, followed by Android phones. Touch became the primary interface, and it transformed personal computing from everyone to everywhere.

In each of these transformations, unknown companies rose from oblivion into greatness, and erstwhile great companies succumbed to oblivion.

GUI interfaces essentially killed WordPerfect and Software Arts, the creators of VisiCalc, two of the top five software companies of the DOS era. Touch interfaces have come close to killing Nokia and BlackBerry phones with their tiny little keys.

There is always overlap between old and new. DOS lasted for a few more years after GUIs before generally disappearing, and there is plenty of work and play still being conducted on desktop Macs and PCs.

Today, the center of our digital lives has moved from the desktop to little devices we carry around. It didn't happen abruptly, nor did everyone migrate simultaneously from one device to the next; instead it occurred just a few minutes here and a few minutes there as we started emailing less and texting more.

We are now at the dawn of the Fourth Transformation. It will move technology from what we carry to what we wear. The user interface will move from a screen you tap to computer-generated images that you actually touch and feel. Instead of inputting with our fingers, we will type much faster with our eyes on virtual keyboards. In previous transformations, it was all about the interface between technology and people; now it becomes all about the *experience*—and that changes nearly everything.

While news coverage may create the impression that this transformation is all happening very fast, it is not yet happening everywhere. In fact, some people and businesses are still trying to adjust to the shift to mobile, the previous transformation. The Fourth Transformation will take a decade to unfold.

It will be driven not just by the rise of new technologies and the simultaneous decline of others, but also by the rise of younger generations and the decline of an older one.

For it to be an authentic transformation, more than technology needs to change; culture must simultaneously adapt. The way people relate to technology must change as must your way of interacting with partners, stakeholders, employees and customers.

Wherever we look, we see a groundswell of such transformative changes taking shape. We see it when we attend HoloLens hackathons where young, passionate developers create augmented reality applications that make our jaws drop—apps that simply won't work on mobile phones or desktops.

We see it when an unknown company located in an unlikely part of the country raises $1.3 billion for a product that doesn't exist, intended for no announced customers. Yet, by the time you read this, Magic Leap will already be a household name or damned close to it.

We see it when we encounter excited people at the Consumer Electronics Show waiting in lines that remind us of those that formed outside Apple Stores when new phones came out. But now they are waiting to try on new VR headsets with new names like HTC Vive or Oculus Rift—names you never heard of until recently.

From a technology perspective, the Fourth Transformation is all about virtual, augmented, and mixed reality (MR). MR glasses will control self-driving cars, drones, robots, and the Internet of Things (IoT), but they will do a lot more than just that: They will blur the lines between that which is real and that which is a computer-generated illusion. Now, instead of sitting and passively watching stuff on screens, we will become immersed and surrounded, wandering freely in and around it.

The digital blood that runs through these new devices, giving them virtual hearts and brains, is artificial intelligence (AI). We write more about the devices than the underpinnings in this book, but the AI is the secret sauce—the great enabler of the Fourth Transformation.

From a business perspective, this transformation is about greater accuracy, productivity, efficiency and safety: an entirely new way for businesses and customers to talk with each other.

On the societal level, it is a better way of learning, of receiving news, of meeting new people and of communicating visually so that everyone understands, rather than just those who speak a particular language. It also marks a period in which machines begin to augment humans and behave more like humans themselves.

It is all this and so much more. It is a fundamental and global transformation.

How do we know? If you are a traditional business person, you want statistics, and we don't have them yet, because stats are built on what has already happened. We have traveled the world to learn about what many of the most talented, passionate and visionary people are developing *right now* as we write this book.

We have also talked to some of the best strategists in retail, the enterprise, health and learning, and they have shared with us projects that they have started—and results that make them cautiously euphoric.

We've observed and talked with our children, grandchildren and other kids we know, because they are the best way we have to understand the near-term future.

We are convinced this Fourth Transformation has begun, and it will change business and life. It is a force that cannot and should not be stopped. It promises a better, healthier, safer, more informative world than the one we have now.

So who is this book for? Why bother to read it?

Primarily, we write books about the near-term future for business decision makers who want to understand technology developments so that they can adjust course. We hope to provide information and ideas that enable businesses to start early with small projects so that they can understand the potential opportunities now.

The challenge of a business decision maker these days is to stay ahead of customers in technology changes—but not too far ahead. We hope this book will give you information and ideas so that you can begin the long, but fast-moving, path into the Fourth Transformation.

We've split this book into three parts:

Part 1 describes changes in technology and people. We talk about how VR is changing games and entertainment, how AR has been alive and useful in the enterprise for years, and how two emergent generations have new attitudes about technology that will change behavior for them as customers, employees and competitors.

Part 2 tells you about changes already going on in four areas of business: retail, the enterprise, health and learning. We also explain how artificial intelligence is changing the way we interact with devices in our personal lives. We call these smart machines *Digital Genies* because our wishes become their demands, but the price we will pay is that they will know more about us than any human in our lives.

Part 3 looks at the big picture, first examining the disturbing possibilities of lost privacy, jobs and the ability to discern truth from illusion. We conclude that, for better or worse, the Fourth Transformation is inevitable, and it is wisest to prepare for it sooner than your competitor and before your first customer walks through your door wearing an MR headset.

One clarifying note: We are two authors. When we tell stories that apply to only one of us, we'll use our last names (Scoble and Israel), just as when we talk about other people.

When you have finished our book, we hope you will have information and ideas that will help you adjust course, so that you and your business will thrive in the coming Fourth Transformation.

Robert Scoble
Shel Israel
November 2016

PART 1

Game Changers

CHAPTER 1
What Zuck Saw

"Some things need to be believed to be seen."

—Guy Kawasaki, Evangelist, Author

In April 2016, Mark Zuckerberg stood before an audience of 1,700 developers, partners and media at F8, Facebook's annual developer conference. Another 100,000 watched online.

Wearing his signature gray T-shirt and blue jeans, clasping a large handheld microphone, he was simultaneously relaxed and passionate. This was among his longest, and many would say his best, talks.

He laid out Facebook's intended path for the next ten years.

About halfway through his presentation, Zuck presented his vision for where technology was going next. He showed a slide of what appeared to be a very ordinary pair of eyeglasses. There was mild applause, but few dropped jaws; the picture just looked like glasses with slightly thick frames, as you might find on the shelf in a Warby Parker store.

But for us, it was a gratifying moment. It confirmed that the head of the world's sixth most valuable company was seeing what we were seeing, and he was declaring that Facebook was shifting its course into the Fourth Transformation. Facebook, like Google, Microsoft, Apple, Sony, Samsung, Snapchat, Nintendo, Lenovo, Alibaba and Tencent, not to mention scores of impressive and well-financed startups, was moving toward a new era where humans and intelligent machines would interact in ways that were first envisioned in science fiction.

To industry insiders, what Zuck said was not all that new. Facebook and the others had been investing heavily in this direction. Behind those ordinary-looking glasses was the best work of some of the world's best thinkers, the biggest investments from some of the world's deepest pockets, solutions to some of the most daunting product design problems and a vision shared by a growing number of people. That vision: A device such as the *smart glasses* Zuck showed would deliver so many benefits that by the year 2025, most people would be using them more than they were using their smartphones in 2016.

All this certainly had not started with Zuck on the stage, and it was not the first time that the world heard about the concept of smart glasses. In 2016, virtual reality (VR) and augmented reality (AR) headsets were already making big news.

VR glasses such Sony PlayStation VR, Oculus Rift and HTC Vive headsets immerse users in artificial worlds. The user's real surroundings are blocked off. Augmented reality enhances what is really around the user with virtual content, such as useful data or entertaining images. With AR, you can tell what is real and what is not.

Mixed reality, such as what Microsoft HoloLens and Meta 2 offer, integrates computer-generated images with what is really there so well that it is hard to tell them apart. VR and AR are essential ingredients in mixed reality. Over time, we predict, that MR will be the prevailing term in an industry that currently has so many terms that it causes confusion.

Smart glasses, will be mixed reality glasses. They will start to resemble what Zuck showed, probably by 2020 or so.

Today's MR glasses, while exciting, are clumsy-looking and relatively expensive. Some are tethered to computer consoles or require you to carry a computer in a backpack. The VR headsets blind you from surrounding reality; wearing them as you walk down the street would make you a candidate for a Darwin Award.

In terms of devices, Zuck's smart glasses are the ultimate goal for enhanced reality devices. People will primarily use them as mixed reality devices, but they may have a VR setting for games, entertainment, learning, health and other applications.

We expect to see them by 2020 at the earliest. But they will ignite a tsunami of adoption. The migration from handsets to headsets will not be like the flick of a switch. Instead, most people will buy the new devices for a single reason, perhaps entertainment or medical assistance, and then will find more and more reasons to use the glasses. They will start moving, a few minutes at a time, from their phones to their glasses.

By 2025, people will be spending far more time with the smart glasses, and the smartest businesses will have shifted their efforts from aging mobile apps to the most innovative MR applications.

Smart Glasses

The lenses of smart glasses will look a lot like simple eyeglasses. People who have optical prescriptions will be able to get them with MR capability. These will contain tiny nano-technological screens that will appear as 90-inch TV screens six feet in front of you, creating an image density eight times greater than HDTV.

There is an especially magic feature at the crux of how smart glasses work. They can take something that is really in your field of view and replace it with computer-generated images that you will be able to actually touch and manipulate.

The computer and graphic processing units, power supplies, Wi-Fi and Bluetooth connections will be inside your eyeglass frames, which will conduct an imperceptible amount of low-wattage electricity. Your glasses will connect wirelessly to the Internet of Things and will use machine learning to get progressively smarter about you. They will conduct transactions either automatically by gestures, by voice command or, overwhelmingly, by simple and natural eye movements.

Smart glasses will, of course, do whatever a smartphone can do today. In fact, millions of people will become familiar with AR and VR on phones long before they even consider buying a head-mounted display (HMD) a computer you wear in front of your eyes.

We believe most people will prefer HMDs to handsets for a variety of reasons: Young people may think they are cooler, knowledge workers because they are more productive as work tools and industrial field workers because working hands free is so much safer. As time goes on, there will be more and more reasons.

Mixed Reality

Today, we are extremely early in the development and applications of the mixed reality technologies, a term we use to describe VR, AR and MR. Most devices still deny users mobility, the most compelling attribute of phones. This will change soon.

Today, the most compelling experiential improvement from these new technologies is the ability to see things in 3D and to become immersed in them, the same way that you experience real life.

The 3D effect is created by stereoscopically overlapping the fields of vision in the left and right lenses, just as in 3D movies. They also employ stereoscopic sounds, which create a sense that you are surrounded by a symphony orchestra, snarling zombies, cattle stampeding or the hauntingly gentle sounds of humpback whales passing by as you virtually swim off a Hawaiian island.

Few who experience these effects for even a few minutes fail to appreciate the imminent promise of this new technology in entertainment, education and communications. In the next few chapters, we will be telling you about a few less obvious but equally promising applications that will change retail, enterprises and classroom training; remove chronic pain without drugs; treat autism, Parkinson's disease, blindness and paralysis; and so much more.

How does it work?

This is a book for business decision makers about complex technologies. We will go as light as we can on technical terms relevant to our story. If you are a technologist, please forgive us if we seem to describe some issues with excessive simplicity.

One important term to understand is *point cloud*. If you don't understand the technology that point clouds represent, you can easily mistake mixed reality technologies for witchcraft.

You have probably seen point clouds in use in movies, or police detective shows like NCIS: Los Angeles, where what you see on a screen—or through a headset—looks like 3D graph paper with green lines on a black background. Then the outlines of objects fill in until you see an entire landscape.

Point clouds take sets of data and convert them into visible virtual objects. Over time, they are getting very fast in converting data into 3D images that precisely render the relationships between you and the objects that surround you.

These point clouds can also project animated or extremely realistic images of things that are not really there. They can be monsters bursting through a wall, virtual celebrity footprints in a store leading you to a coveted pair of shoes, or a 3D manual that shows which wire to snip to stop a bomb from detonating. They can make a fighter pilot's plane virtually disappear so that she can see an incoming missile pointed her way. More pragmatically, this is how you can look at a couch or model kitchen in an Ikea or a Lowe's and see how it will look in your home.

Point clouds power nearly everything in enhanced reality.

Spatial Computing

Transformations start at one point and lead to another. Today our smartphones are the centers of our digital lives. This is our starting point. Over the next ten years, we will move from these omnipresent handsets to MR headsets that look like what Zuck showed.

They will be mobile and self-contained. They steer the course through the story we are about to tell you, but they are not the destination.

The new era, *spatial computing*, will take ten years to arrive and will last for perhaps 50 more. Spatial computing is the concept that computers can learn the contextual implications of location and the relationships of objects to each other through point clouds.

These objects can include people, who can thus interact with computer-generated objects as well as real things. In spatial computing, you no longer have to sit and watch; you can interact, walk around virtual objects and see the space in a room in the same way as when you walk into any real room. You can set a virtual chessboard on a real table, and have a holographic opponent glare at you and ponder moves from the other side.

The concept of spatial computing has been around in scientific academia for over 50 years. There seems to be no single point of origin. Instead, its roots can be found back in the very dry white papers that Dr. Gordon Moore must have studied when he developed Moore's Law, which predicted that processor densities and speeds would double every two years.

This has remained true since about 1970 when Moore's Law was first introduced. It certainly prevailed since the third transformation, which took us from pointing and clicking on a desktop device to the mobile era, where the starting point was the freedom to hold real-time conversations while moving around.

Think of what has happened to the mobile device since then. Ten years prior to today, the iPhone had not yet been introduced. The BlackBerry and Nokia were hot products in 2006 because they had dependable email and text clients, the first mobile phones to actually do so.

As you think of what has been accomplished in mobile in the past ten years, imagine how far we can go over the next ten years. Think also of how digital technology has changed you and your work in the past ten years. Now think of how it can change your life and work in the next ten.

If you are old enough to remember, ten years ago you marveled that you could talk and text and email on a mobile device. You may not have been able to picture how far you would come in a decade.

The technologies we are about to tell you about in this book are like the BlackBerry and Nokia devices back then. In researching this book, what we found made our jaws drop, and we cannot help but marvel about where it will all go.

Loving and Graceful

We will focus on devices and transformation on the road to spatial computing, but there is one other aspect you should keep in mind as you read this and that is artificial intelligence (AI): digital technologies that perform tasks that traditionally required human intelligence, such as visual perception, speech recognition, decision-making and language translation.

Until recently, only developers could develop AI. More recent breakthroughs allow computers to teach themselves by observing and collecting data, without the bottleneck of programming.

The tech community has begun to replace the term artificial intelligence with machine learning, which, we agree, is a better term. For the sake of variety, we will use both.

Machine learning is what makes devices seem eerily humanlike at times. John Markoff, the *New York Times'* Pulitzer Prize-winning reporter, wrote a book about its implications called *Machines of Loving Grace*, a title that we find ironically accurate.

For this book, machine learning is important because it is the underpinning of the technology that carries people into the Fourth Transformation. It is how machines talk about us with each other, ordering supplies and adjusting thermostats or choosing TV programs on our behalf.

We'll talk about the grace and love in later chapters—as well as some of the unintended consequences and some potentially deliberate abuses. We include an entire chapter called *What Could Possibly Go Wrong?*, and it is the longest chapter in the book.

The Visual Web

One other aspect of what is coming is that these technologies will use words less and visual media more, a point that marketers and communicators need to consider as they move forward into the Fourth Transformation.

In October 2015, Ambarish Mitra published a thought piece in which he predicted a new *Visual Web*, 100 times larger than today's Internet. This move to more visual media is behind what Zuck was talking about and what business strategists are planning for. It also factors into the inevitability that your customers will be communicating with you and each other visually.

Mitra is CEO of Blippar, an image recognition platform for mobile devices. Born in an urban slum in India, he is a successful entrepreneur who ultimately hopes to connect all people, just as Zuck has stated he intends to do. Both also have ambitious business strategies at the heart of their altruistic-sounding strategies.

Mitra believes that AR overcomes the economic barriers of language. On the Visual Web, people will buy and sell things online, wordlessly, by image recognition.

Here's how it will eventually work: A merchant who speaks no Western language has something unique to sell, perhaps an artisan work from someone nearby. He has a cellphone with an Internet connection, but how does he offer it to buyers like you when he speaks no English and you don't speak his native tongue?

The answer is to search by visual images instead of words. There may be 200 ways to say bicycle or bracelet in the world. But a single photo or iconic image can do the job. Thus a local merchant gains access to global markets and global marketers gain access to customers in emerging markets where the most business growth will occur over the next decade, according to *Euromonitor*.

We like the business side of this. On another level it reminds us of the philosopher Immanuel Kant, who essentially argued that countries that conduct trade with each other very rarely go to war against each other, and these days we seem to need more of that.

Blippar is just one of several companies that have become popular by offering free mobile apps focused on visual content, along with ones you may know better such as Instagram, Pinterest and Snapchat.

Blippar uses camera phones and AI to understand and identify objects the way the human brain does; it is machine learning in action. Mitra says when it started out in 2011, Blippar had the recognition abilities of a two-year-old child. It could just learn to differentiate tables from floor, so it knew where to put things. Today, that child has the recognition ability of an eight-year-old, and a decade from now it will have the wisdom of a sage village elder, he told us.

Mitra is far from alone in perceiving the rising tide of video.

Gary Vaynerchuck, who wrote eight books, not to mention our Foreword, told us, "The single most important strategy in content marketing today is video. Whether it's video on Facebook, Twitter, Snapchat or YouTube, the content you need to be thinking about creating and marketing on social for your business is video. Period."

At F8, Zuck also declared a new "Golden Age of Video."

To illustrate the progression, he showed developers a video of his daughter taking her first baby steps. Then he showed a photo his parents had snapped, when he had taken his first step. He guessed that when his parents were born, family and friends got to share the news via words.

His point was that technology is driving people to video because it communicates more information more easily. The tools have gotten better and cheaper; bandwidth and storage may remain an irritant, but they are no longer a major barrier.

Just look at what's happening in 3D video. Just a couple of years ago, professional 3D camera technicians lugged around a heavy rack carrying six cameras that weighed a good deal and could cost nearly $100,000. This year, the GoPro Hero 4 came out offering six professional quality 3D cameras in a sphere you could hold in your hand—or hang from a drone to shoot surfers and skiers in action. Priced at $6,000, it produces the same quality video as the old big and clumsy cameras produced.

Also in 2016, the first batch of consumer-level 3D camera devices came to market, including the Cube 360, which sells for about $80. The quality isn't what you would call great, and it would be insulting to GoPro if we were to compare the two products today.

But consumer quality gets better; it always gets better. Do you remember how crappy the first cameras in phones were? They are still not professional quality, but they are good enough for most people as is evidenced by the success of Instagram, Facebook and Snapchat. It is good enough for an artisan living on a dirt floor in sub-Saharan Africa to sell woven baskets and pottery to homeowners on Long Island or in Hong Kong who want something unique at an attractive price.

The Visual Web breaks down cultural barriers. As it develops, it creates entrepreneurial opportunities that challenge brand marketers who do not adjust course.

One last thought: It is faster and easier to take pictures and videos when you are using a head-mounted device rather than one you have to pull out of your pocket or purse to use.

Pistol Shot

Facebook is one of many powerful and capable players redirecting technology and the people who use it toward the Fourth Transformation and ultimately into the Age of Spatial Computing, where most of us will be wearing intelligent machines that are far more mobile and capable than today's generation.

We do not know—nor do we consider it particularly important—what companies and products will win or lose. Ultimately we write to business decision makers as end user champions.

We are entering a time of great competition, which has always driven innovation while lowering price—two constant results of Moore's law.

What is important to us and you about what Zuck did when he showed that slide is this: He fired a pistol shot telling the world that times were going to inalterably change.

It means that life and business as usual will become unusual and that customers will expect new kinds of experiences when they shop with you or talk with you as investors or partners.

It means that companies you have never heard of will get their own shot at a position in the new world order of spatial computing.

We know that some investors got Zuck's message. Eric Romo, founder of Silicon Valley-based AltspaceVR, a social VR startup that we'll discuss in the next chapter, told us that before Zuck's comments he could not raise a dime, but after Zuck spoke he got a deal that he liked with relative speed and ease.

Before Zuck showed his slide, the conversations were about *the possibility* of these new headsets. After, conversations shifted to the *inevitability* of them. For the passionate and nascent industry, Zuck provided a confirmation that the vision may start with virtual, but it is not a hallucination; it is already becoming reality.

One last thing about that shot: Zuck's bullet was virtual, so it did no damage.

To start, let's see what is happening with VR, which is the only enhanced reality technology to reach consumers in great numbers so far. While VR applications are not all just fun and games, that's where it starts, and it may have more impact on your business than you realize.

+++++

CHAPTER 2

Minecraft Generation

"We shape our tools and thereafter they shape us."

—attributed to Marshall McLuhan, communication theorist

The tools of change started to roll out at approximately the same time as Zuck spoke in April 2016. There was, of course, Facebook's own Oculus Rift, but there were also HTC Vive, Sony PlayStation VR, Samsung Gear VR, Google Cardboard and numerous others receiving less attention.

If these were the first digital weapons of the next revolution, the evidence indicated that the new disruption would be fun, and the soldiers would be gamers whose combat skills allowed them to traverse computer-animated landscapes, while avoiding booby traps and zapping zombies.

Technically, the new headsets are called HMDs—or *head-mounted displays*. They are extremely sophisticated and make two important changes in your perception.

First, when you use an HMD, it sees what you see at the same time. Second, instead of sitting in front of the screen watching action behind it, you become immersed in what you see. It is all around you. The screen is no longer a barrier.

It is also important to note that the devices getting so much attention today are the first forays into the Fourth Transformation; they are just the starting point. What they look like now and what they can do today may be dazzling compared with yesterday, but a few years from now they will seem primitive, the way an MS-DOS screen or a mechanical mouse seems to us today.

As we write, the price for the best VR devices is $800, but these need to be attached to a computer that is turbocharged with a pricey, high-performance graphics card. Every product has glitches that the makers promise to improve in future versions, yet every product being offered is selling out, and their manufacturers are struggling to fulfill backlog orders.

Most significantly, as we write this, not one of the devices is mobile, a problem which must be solved if this Fourth Transformation is to reach its promise.

So what's the big deal? It comes down to a single word: *experience*. There is simply nothing like what happens when you put on a headset.

When people first put one on, they immediately step into a strange and wondrous environment, one that exceeds their own imaginations. It's as if they have climbed through a window directly into a world that they previously had to watch from outside. Instead of just watching, they become immersed. VR has been likened to LSD, except what you see is created by studios, not chemicals.

VR headsets let you journey into far-off worlds while remaining relatively stationary in a room, often tethered to a computer console. If gaming software is involved, then *you become the game*. If it's a storytelling adventure, you control the script; the story does not unfold as a director dictates, but according to where you choose to look. You are in control: You are the story, and no one gets to see it precisely as you do, even when they are playing or watching with you.

When people first try on a VR headset, they are startled by the experience. When it is over, they usually want more, even *crave* more. After people buy headsets, they almost immediately share what they have experienced with friends—igniting what Charlene Li and Josh Bernoff described as a groundswell in their 2011 book. Their friends buy headsets and share them with more friends who buy headsets.

People who make these devices rarely advertise. Instead, they set up demo kiosks at shows, conferences and public gathering places where more people try them for ten minutes, then buy, then share with friends, adding to the groundswell.

VR is like nothing that has preceded it. It is exciting, creative and fun. Zuck called it the most social platform he has seen; on our last day of writing this book, he announced that the next version of his Oculus VR headsets would become more social—and more mobile.

If Zuck is right about what he sees coming, then VR, AR and MR will ultimately converge into one chic device and the gadgets receiving breathless reviews today will be relegated to museums.

Mainstreaming Millennials

Technology change does not happen uniformly. It starts with a group of early adopters and spreads from there. The coming changes in VR, AR, and mixed reality start with Millennials and those who are younger. But they will spread from there to people of all ages and cultures.

Millennials are the first generation of digital natives. What will future generations of digital natives be like? How should you plan to reach them as customers? What will you use to attract the best of them as employees? What will the most entrepreneurial of them do to compete with established organizations such as yours?

To understand Millennials, watch them at play—and watch who and what they play with. Play shapes who they become. Their toys are indicative of how later in life they will learn, socialize, solve problems and conduct their work. If you want your business to be relevant to them, then you need to understand the impact that mixed reality technologies will have on them early in life.

Just as Boomers were the first generation to grow up watching TV and it shaped who they became, Millennials were the first generation to grow up with touching mobile phone screens and that has shaped who they have become.

One last point about Millennials. Sometimes older people think of them as if they were children who will eventually grow up and behave more like their elders. That isn't going to happen. Millennials are already beyond college age. There are more of them in the marketplace today than there are aging Boomers, and they will be a business factor for you over the next 50 years.

And how they play today is the best hint you have at reaching them as shoppers, employees and competitors.

According to *VentureBeat*, today's average gamer is 31 years old. She or he came of age in the Great Recession at the start of the new century. While these young gamers are reputed to be financially constrained and budget-minded, they somehow are finding resources to buy pricey gaming devices such as Microsoft Xbox, Sony PlayStation or Windows-based PCs souped-up with powerful Nvidia graphics cards.

What drives this behavior is not the tech itself, it is the experience. The desire for the best experience has motivated them to buy the best possible smartphones, and now they are the generation driving adoption for VR headsets.

The HTC Vive, the most expensive of the VR devices released so far, sold 15,000 headsets in its first ten minutes of availability, closing its first day of sales with a significant backlog. Millennials are driving sales for Oculus Rift and other VR headsets so far.

One last thing about gamers: There are *a lot* of them.

Venturewire estimated there were 1.2 billion gamers worldwide in 2016. Eighty percent of all US homes contain game-playing devices, with an average of two players in every home, according to the Entertainment Software Association (ESA).

These are the people who will be buying the VR headsets, and if you are fortunate, they will also be your customers. If Millennial gamers like whatever it is you sell, then we are bullish about your future. The best thing for you to do now, however, is to start thinking about the new headsets and how they can improve your customer experiences.

The early evidence indicates that VR adoption will come faster and be bigger than laptops, smartphones or anything that has preceded it. If you adopt them in your store or workplace to enhance experiences, then you would be making a wise move now that will favorably shape the future.

By the year 2025, we believe there will be several hundred million people with either VR headsets or the mixed reality smart glasses we told you about in Chapter 1.

When will the moment come when there are more people using smart glasses than smartphones? Our guess is that this will happen not later than 2025. Most people won't even notice their transformation, just as we didn't notice the day when we started using our phones more than our computers.

Cannibalizing the Traditional

Of course, not all computer gamers are Millennials. They skew into all age brackets and can be found in both senior housing and day care centers. Like technology, the habits and expectations of gamers are constantly in motion.

Demographers cite various start dates between 1976 and 1982 for the births of Millennials, with a majority going for 1976. If you use that as the start year, then ten years from today, many Millennials will be parents and some will even be grandparents. How will Fourth Transformation technology play into their family culture? Will grandparents play VR games with the toddlers, at holidays and get-togethers, the way our grandparents played horseshoes with us?

Of course they will. The new headsets will be as central to family connection and culture as phones are today.

In fact, there is already a new generation of digital natives emerging and becoming more significant as a market demographic every day.

Minecraft Generation

The next generation will be raised even more digitally than the Millennials they follow. According to Sparks and Honey, a U.S.-based consultancy, in 2014, 41% of this new generation spent more than three hours daily using computers for purposes other than schoolwork—about double the time Millennials spent at the same age. We assume that much of it is spent in games and in social activities—which are increasingly one and the same.

This new generation will enter grade school using digital devices to play, learn and socialize. Sociologists say they are more comfortable with technology than Millennials.

Well so what? If you run an automotive company or a travel agency, or if you chart the course for a community college or manage a mall, why should you care about kids and digital games?

If your marketing people are not thinking about Fourth Transformation technologies, then you will not get their attention. If your merchandisers are not thinking about how AR will help people find what they want in your stores, younger generations will shop elsewhere.

If you do not provide the new tools in your workplace, then the brightest of them will not choose to work for you, and the most aggressive of their entrepreneurs will see you as competitive pushovers.

Demographers are sociologists who study populations. This data-driven vocation produces the stuff that modern marketing depends on to determine what to say and how to say it. They usually get to name a new generation, based on a single factor that drives social behavior.

Sometimes they do well, as when they came up with *The Greatest Generation* as the name for people who grew up in the Great Depression and then fought—and won—World War 2. Sometimes, they draw creative blanks, as with *Generation X.*

This emerging second generation of digital natives has proven tough for them to name: They've tried: *iGens, Post-Millennials, Centennials* and the unfathomable *Plurals.* Lately, they seem to have settled on *Gen Z*, sometimes shortened to *Zees.*

We don't like any of these. The letter 'Z' implies finality, yet this generation to us represents more of a beginning: They will be the first to come of age in the Fourth Transformation, and we think the culture they shape will be defined by a single compelling game that so many of them play, a game that centers on living and building in a virtual world.

So we call them the *Minecraft Generation*, or *Minecrafters* for short.

Natural vs Acquired

In *Lethal Generosity*, Shel Israel's previous book, he wrote about Millennials being more comfortable with digital devices than Boomers. He talked about the differences between naturally *acquiring* versus consciously *learning* languages. Everyone starts acquiring at least one language before age 5. They have them pretty much down pat by the time they enter grade school, and they, of course, grow up speaking like the natives that they are.

It turns out that children can acquire one, two or more languages and speak them like natives—providing they learn them before reaching puberty. We have no idea why puberty triggers how languages are learned, but that is what scientists say.

When we try to learn post-puberty, we are likely to speak languages with accents, no matter how proficient we become in vocabulary. As hard as we try, we will never speak as natives.

The mental processes involved in learning computers and computer languages turns out to be identical to learning natural languages. Learning to use these tools as children makes the tools more organic, and learning them when you are older requires harder work. No matter how proficient we become, we won't think digitally the way younger learners do.

In our view, the relationships Millennials and Minecrafters have with digital technology defines their respective generations and differentiates them from all preceding generations.

The difference between Millennials and Minecrafters is not so clear. But we think it is that Millennials are adept at talking to each other through technology, while Minecrafters are adept at speaking with the technology itself. Like generations that came before them, Minecrafters learn many languages; what is different is that one of their most popular languages is coding.

Minecrafters make coding a universal language. This eliminates barriers of doing business across multi-lingual borders just as Blippar and others will do it with the Visual Web.

Digital Hopscotch

Some games, of course, stayed unchanged for centuries, as children play games in pretty much the same way their parents and grandparents did. For example, Hopscotch goes back to ancient Egypt. Modern kids play an adaptation that goes back to Rome where soldiers picked it up after invading Egypt.

But now, a version of Hopscotch has become a computer game, one of many that teaches children to code. They use this language to create games of their own, which they share with other elementary and preschool children, in an online global community. Hopscotch makes it easy for other kids to play for free or to borrow strings of code to develop games of their own, which, in turn, they share as well.

Scoble's kids Ryan and Milan are seven and nine, respectively, as we write. As Minecrafters, they have not known a world without smartphones and tablets. When they want to try a new game, they don't turn to their parents for guidance or permission, they go to YouTube, learn about a game, choose and download it. This is a culture change in that kids learn to do things for themselves in more ways, more often.

When Scoble's kids were first introduced to a VR headset this year, they needed a minute of instruction on operating the hand controllers, but they intuitively knew what to do when they put them on. When they become shoppers, do you think AR or VR might be a useful strategy for gaining their interest or loyalty?

Before Minecrafters enter grade school, they are using digital technology to become makers, to become more self-reliant, and to find and socialize with other kids. Before they enter high school, tens of millions of them will be playing VR and AR games. Perhaps they will start on phones, but we figure that will just make them want headsets more.

Such generational characteristics create the sort of open culture that Zuckerberg referred to at F8.

The idea of the world's children ignoring the inherent boundaries of geography, religion and politics to play together is an image we love, one that has hope built into it. They speak in a universal language called code, a transcendent language that transcends differences.

Many other games and sites teach code. Perhaps a decade from today, more people will communicate in binary code than in English.

The most popular of these games is, of course, the game after which we named the Minecraft Generation.

From 15 to a billion?

Minecraft is history's best-selling PC video game and is also among the most popular games on phones and consoles. In February 2015, *GameSpot* estimated Minecraft had 100 million registered users and the adoption rate was rising.

All this grew from an inauspicious start in 2009, when founder Markus Persson offered unfinished versions online for $10 each. In the first day he received 15 takers and was ecstatic. Microsoft acquired the game in 2014, giving it the resources to scale.

The basic game starts on a sparsely developed virtual world, where players mine minerals, extracting precious metals for currency and carving the rest into blocks for constructing walls, buildings, robots or whatever they choose.

There are few rules, and besides, players can ignore them if they choose.

There are dozens of versions that sell for about $20 a pop. Often, these are derived through partnerships with popular brands such as *Jurassic Park, Transformers* and Disney. Through a partnership with Lego, players can build tangible models of what they first built on Minecraft online—or they can just use a 3D printer.

Although a significant minority of Minecraft players choose to play alone, most enjoy multiuser versions; this is a community that likes to share what they create, particularly on YouTube, where—the last time we checked—there were over 150 million uploads by kids sharing their work so that others can get new ideas, which they, in turn, may choose to share with *YouTube's* robust Minecraft community.

Computer gaming overall is as open source a community as exists anywhere. Competing game publishers readily borrow ideas and code from each other with nary a squawk about proprietary rights, according to *Wired* magazine.

As in other computer games, Minecraft players regularly share—and hack—code.

Minecraft has built a culture indifferent to borders. It teaches the advantages of collaboration to solve problems.

In May 2016, Minecraft shipped VR versions for Oculus Rift and Samsung Gear and announced plans for an AR version on Microsoft's own HoloLens.

This port of a game is also a bridge from an established technology to a newer one. Minecrafters and whatever generation follows them will be using AR/VR/MR technologies before they enter kindergarten. They are going to expect it to be available to them when they shop, where they work, where they live and in their entertainment.

What starts in games does not stay in games. What is being played at home today will shape your business in the near tomorrow.

Spilling Over

Games drive innovation. They helped drive adoption of the mouse, computer graphics, PC sound, chat and online communities.

So much of modern personal technology can be tracked back to games. It isn't just the software. It's also the chips, screens, storage and bandwidth. History shows that where gamers take people, everything else follows.

There is another powerful cultural phenomenon that is about to change even more profoundly than games.

We refer to the ancient art of storytelling.

+++++

CHAPTER 3

Virtual Storytelling

"You're traveling through another dimension, a dimension not only of sight and sound, but of mind—a journey into a wondrous land whose boundaries are that of imagination."

—Rod Serling, The Twilight Zone

There is something about humans that loves a good story. It goes back to our earliest recorded times. In fact, storytelling is how we record our history.

Picture, if you will, a cave-dwelling clan of early Cro-Magnon times. They had few tools and used them for the most basic activities such as hunting, holding stuff or fire starting. So here's a story about them:

One day, the hunters return from a journey dragging a freshly killed creature. Their arrival brings great joy—for now there will be food to survive the winter.

That night, the entire clan prepares and enjoys a great feast. The celebration is enhanced by alcoholic beverages, which have been recently invented. As the night wears on, the fire turns to embers and celebrants settle down. Someone encourages the leader of the hunt to tell what happened.

With a limited vocabulary of grunts illustrated by gestures, he describes the adventure, exaggerating only the hazards and struggle. At one point, frustrated that words won't describe what he wants, he picks up a stick and draws in the cave's dirt floor.

He draws and the others smile and are impressed as the sketch enlightens them as words could not do. There is laughter, plus abundant oohs and ahs.

The plentiful food and drink have an effect: One-by-one clan members drift into sleep, except for one who is perhaps too small or young to hunt.

Her mind overflows with visions inspired by the story. As the others sleep, she crushes some soft rocks and mixes the crude powder with a little blood from the felled beast and gathered berries for color.

Then she paints a few crude pictures of the story on the cave wall. In the morning, the others pause to admire the work and to praise her, then they go about their tasks. The years go by and what with the saber-toothed beasts, hostile neighboring clans, infection and nasty weather, the tribe thins, then disappears entirely.

All that is left is the cave drawing.

Four thousand years go by, and then a hiker stumbles into the cave and uncovers the drawings that had remained. The scientists come, and they determine certain facts by carbon dating the embers left by the clan. They scrape DNA from charred bones. Remnants in a broken stone urn confirm it once contained fermented liquid.

There are news reports and films and books about the discovery. Some people take note, and what most will remember are the pictures on the wall, pictures that have some resemblance to the ones their daughters made with crayons that are now displayed on refrigerator doors.

Stories endure long after the narrators are gone. The names of the best storytellers remain even after they become dust. Who among us would recognize Aesop or Shakespeare or Orwell, if they were sitting next to us on a commuter jet?

We made up this particular story to illustrate the cultural ties to stories which are the foundation of religion, patriotism and inspirations. Stories pervade books, opera, movies and comics. Elders still sit around campfires and tell tales to thrill and scare youngsters. True stories are related and enhanced by the narrators who make the fish they caught larger and the monsters of darkness fiercer.

That brings us to virtual reality, a descendant of the clan girl's cave drawings as well as of the scientists and technologists who investigated their discovery. VR software is a product both of the ancient art of story telling and the most advanced applications of digital technology.

We talk a lot in this book of how the lines of truth and illusion are blurring. People express concern about this phenomenon, perhaps rightfully so, but humans have been blurring truth and illusion for thousands of years. Now we have a cooler, more immersive, entertaining and memorable way of doing it.

VR is more experiential than anything that has preceded it. If we had used VR instead of written words to tell you our story, you would have felt the damp of the cave and the warmth of the fire, with the help of haptic sensors, as the story unfolded. You would have focused on the gesturing hands of the hunter and looked over the shoulder of the artist who painted on the wall. Instead of sitting and watching the story, you would be *immersed* in it.

Let's look at all the ways that is happening these days.

Painting in Midair

For about 2,400 years, Aristotle defined the primary rule for how all stories must be structured: They must have a beginning, a middle and an end. This sounds blatantly obvious on the surface of it.

But if you think about it, our real life stories never unfold that way.

Very often, we don't know when a personal episode actually starts, and we may be surprised to discover who the principal players really are. We don't quite know when a chapter—never mind the entire story—has ended. Even when someone abruptly dies, that is not the end to it. There are legal matters to manage, estates to settle, stories about the loved one to pass on to younger family members.

Life is just too ad hoc to conform to Aristotle's rules.

There's a second issue having to do with a term almost as ancient as Aristotle: *Solipsism* is the belief that each of us is the center of his or her own universe. Stories, as we come to know them, will unfold based on where we are and where we choose to look. Bob Dylan expressed it well in an early song: "I'll let you be in my stories, if I can be in yours."

Let's look at how this will work in cinema.

Shari Frilot is curator of the experimental New Frontiers section of the *Sundance Film Festival*, which she dedicated to VR in 2016. Her three finalists each received rave reviews, the favorite being *Dear Angelica*, produced by Oculus Story Studio.

The movie's protagonist is Jessica and the 360-degree video of *Dear Angelica* reveals memories of her recently deceased mother. In a review of the experience posted on *The Verge*, Adi Robertson wrote that after putting on a headset, all she could see was a single word:

> Hello. From the front, it looks like ordinary cursive, but using the Rift's tracking camera, I can walk to the side and see the letters collapse into a tangle of meaningless black loops.
>
> A few moments later, the world's white background begins to fill with three-dimensional illustrations. They fade in, line-by-line, a cloud-streaked sky being navigated by a sleek flying dragon, carrying two small figures on its back. It's like a painting that floats in midair.
>
> [That's a pretty strong review considering that Robertson was only watching the pre-roll credits.] In any other medium, what Oculus has brought to Sundance this year would be called storyboard or concept art. But in VR, it's extraordinary.

In a later scene, the reviewer finds herself reading over Jessica's shoulder as the character composes a letter to her deceased mother. Robertson's focus wanders off as she admires the room's furniture. The character keeps on writing, oblivious of the voyeur-in-a-headset.

When *Dear Angelica* is released in Fall 2016, general audiences will immerse themselves in the finished film at their own pace, wandering off into whatever directions and sequences they choose. Two people who attend and view together may leave with decidedly different perspectives on what they experienced or what the central point was.

Mainstream studios are planning the same sort of changes to film productions.

In late 2015, Scoble visited Ted Schilowitz, 20th Century Fox's futurist, who showed him a clip from *Wild*, the Reese Witherspoon film being adapted to VR. As Scoble watched the star hiking along the Pacific Crest Trail, he turned around to encounter, to his surprise, a second hiker, not present in the released version of the film.

That experience helped us to understand why the technology has to watch what the user watches. *Dear Angelica's* reviewer turned to examine furniture; Scoble turned to encounter a second actor.

Not only did technology change the story. It also changed the viewer experience. Perhaps, in a few small ways, it changes the viewer.

When it comes to children, that change might be deeper and more profound.

Updating Timeless Tales

Some children's stories have remained unchanged for centuries. Penrose, a studio founded by Eugene Chung, an Oculus Rift co-founder, uses VR to modernize all-time favorites. *The Rose and I*, Penrose's VR adaptation of *The Little Prince*, also debuted at Sundance to acclaim.

Later in 2016, Penrose released trailers for *Allumette*, based on *The Little Matchstick Girl*. Both films create a sense in viewers that they are giants looking in on miniature players the way a child might see toy figures inside a dollhouse.

There is an age factor here. Children are particularly accepting of AR and VR, and so are most viewers who are younger than 35. Most people do not change their tastes much after they reach their 35th birthday; they continue with the preferences they formed earlier in their lives. This will likely be true of kids being exposed to new technologies so early in life. Projecting forward, more people will prefer the new forms of entertainment, even as those who reject the change carry their disdain to their graves.

Culture will change. People will arrive at the Cinema 19 at the mall and have a choice of watching in VR glasses in one theater and without them in another. Over time the glassless theater will get smaller, then eventually disappear.

Five years from now, the Academy Awards will have new categories for VR films as well as the traditional style. The ones that do not have VR effects will appeal to older, diminishing audiences. Non-VR films will be relegated to minor categories like foreign language and documentary films.

The new approaches have already started to inspire live theater as well.

Curious in the Night

The Curious Incident of the Dog in the Night Time tells the story of a mathematically gifted autistic boy, wrongly accused of killing a neighbor's dog. To prove his innocence, he sets out to find the culprit. *Curious* received the Tony for best new play of 2015.

In this play, performed on a bare stage, all the props, settings and special effects are created by something akin to virtual reality, so theatergoers can enjoy the performance without wearing headsets.

The set's black, LED-lighted walls visually transform from one scene to the next as they become classroom blackboards, neighborhood streets, trains, outer space and the inner psyche of a troubled mind. Sometimes, actors take a break backstage and the quasi VR gives a captivating solo performance.

While *Curious* uses the visual marvels of virtual worlds without immersing people in them, a different New York play captures VR's immersive experience without actually using the technology or, for that matter, an actual theater.

Sleep No More is a remake of Shakespeare's *Macbeth*. It arrived in New York City eight years after opening in London, before anyone used the words *VR* and *theater* in the same sentence. *Sleep* is more of an outgrowth of the Environmental Theaters of the '60s where ticket holders followed actors along the sidewalks of New York into a series of physical settings.

Sleep is unlike any Macbeth you have experienced. For one thing, while actors utter a few lines to people watching them, there is no scripted dialog between players—kind of radical for a Shakespeare adaptation. For another, it takes place in the dimly lit McKittrick Hotel, which is actually a converted empty SOHO warehouse.

Attendees walk at their own pace randomly from one scene into another.

VR technology pioneers encouraged us to see the show because they said that *Sleep No More* influenced them in creating VR narrative.

After seeing it, here's what Scoble wrote:

"What's the lesson of this play for the VR world? The action happens all around. Over there is a fight. Over here, is a love scene playing out. Some scenes are so personal that you are required to watch them alone. They split up couples who walked in together, saying it must be experienced alone. The stage is all around you, and you walk through, much like you will in the VR movies that are coming."

Vomiting Visitors

Entertainment and technology keep changing the possibilities for how stories can be told. Here's one about a movie you have probably seen, that became a play you possibly saw, and now is producing a VR version you really should see.

The Lion King, a Disney production that opened on Broadway in 2006, is based on the 1994 movie. It uses humans to replace the original animated characters, and now *Circle of Life*, the celebrated opening segment, is being converted into a VR property.

Disney contracted Total Cinema 360, a VR software and filmmaking studio, to produce *Circle* in the Minskoff Theater where the live play was continuing into its tenth year. The producers wanted to capture the energy of a live performance for the virtual version. In the VR-enhanced format, viewers will experience *Circle* from the perspective of orchestra seats, center stage, backstage and from the wings.

Andrew Flatt, Disney's senior VP of marketing, told the *LA Times* he sees the new property as an experiment that could benefit other Broadway plays. VR can create exciting trailers, where viewers will sense the full thrill of the live production and will thus want to attend. We're sure smart marketers will start using VR to preview all sorts of events.

Disney may be the largest corporate investor in VR and is using it on multiple fronts, including serving as lead investor in a $65 million round for Jaunt, a high-profile VR cinema startup that has produced clips for *ABC News* and pro tennis matches for ESPN.

Walt Disney Imagineering (WDI), the division whose slogan is "We make the magic," has developed proprietary VR technology to rebuild *everything* that Disney builds in VR, particularly hotels and theme parks.

WDI has developed facilities in the back lot at Florida's Epcot Center and in facilities at Glendale, California, where they are creating high-definition VR properties.

Mark Mine, founder and director of the Creative Technology Studio (CTS), part of WDI in Glendale, told *Fortune* the 4K technology—four times the density of a standard HDTV screen—allows teams in the Florida and California studios to perfectly synch computer graphics so that the two groups, separated by over 3,000 miles, can simultaneously analyze and understand designs in precisely the same way.

The studio is using VR in virtual models for design and architecture, not only saving time and money, but also allowing those who create spaces to experience what guests will experience before a hotel room or park attraction is actually built.

In a massive undertaking, WDI used VR to design the $5.5 billion Shanghai Disneyland which opened in September 2016. Also in the works are *Avatar Land* for Orlando and a new Hong Kong Disneyland, as well as *Star Wars* for multiple properties.

Universal Studios, the No. 2 theme park developer, has set up VR attractions based at its parks for such major amusements as *Harry Potter, Transformers* and *Iron Man*. By the time you read this, Universal probably will have fixed a latency problem causing some visitors on the Hollywood Harry Potter ride to vomit.

Theme parks with lower budgets use VR, but in more modest ways. Six Flags Magic Mountain has added VR headsets to the roller coaster, on which passengers will now travel through Superman's Metropolis while the man of steel saves the city from 3D bad guys.

Many pro sports teams including the Golden State Warriors, New England Patriots, San Francisco Giants and Sacramento Kings have created places for fans to use VR to see how it enhances the game. The Boston Red Sox, for example, have a virtual dugout for fans to enjoy.

The Void Enters

A VR theme park chain that started from scratch in March 2016 aspires to compete by creating facilities at low cost, in short periods of time with more VR thrills.

The Void is the first native-VR theme park chain. Curtis Hickman, co-founder and creative director, described the new theme parks as a "vision of infinite dimensions" when he previewed them at the TED conference in Vancouver in January 2016.

The Void is setting up VR experience centers in urban warehouses throughout North America. They feature a series of rooms large enough to hold eight 30-foot-square areas to accommodate diverse adventures. Haptic technology provides visitors a sense of touch so you can experiences the wetness of an ocean floor or the heat of a volcano; they also let you feel the touch and warmth of a real or holographically produced virtual person.

In each center, there will be a variety of experiential rooms. One features a Mayan Temple spewing flames that visitors have the dubious pleasure of feeling through haptic technology enabled by 22 sensors in their vests. In another, experience-seekers will pay to save the world by zapping alien bad guys.

In summer of 2016, *The Void* premiered *Ghostbusters Dimension* in VR at Madame Tussauds New York, in conjunction with Sony Pictures, which had just released the movie. Visitors strapped on ghost-busting photon packs and toted guns equipped with haptic sensors.

Scoble was among those who visited. Team members communicated with each other and collaborated on how best to bust ghosts. "I felt the rumble of the ghost blasting devices and the ghosts themselves when they passed through me. I experienced heat, wet and other sensations. It was the most immersive experience I have had so far, and it was also the most social," he said.

And yet, each of the eight team members had a unique adventure, experiencing it as their own solipsistic adventure. As Bob Dylan said, they were in each other's stories, yet each was their own star.

There is a growing technology toolkit of accessories that can help you feel inside VR in new ways. We've seen guns where you feel the kick, seats you use to navigate, and the Subpac vest that lets you feel impacts like a music beat or a virtual punch in an action game.

Headsets in the Stadium

In 2015, the NFL took in $12 billion. But the stadium competes not only with other pro and amateur teams, but also with local sports taverns that, as Robert Kraft, CEO of the New England Patriots told us in *Age of Context*, offer free HDTV and lower-priced beers usually served faster.

In that book, we also wrote about how football and baseball stadiums had installed sensors to do everything from letting season ticket holders order beers by mobile app, to viewing customizable replays and close-ups on their phones. Contextual technologies even help fans find the restrooms with the shortest lines.

Into this mix now comes Fourth Transformation technologies, and fan experience seems to be getting high priority. Several stadiums have established special augmented reality viewing platforms where fans take turns looking at games through AR headsets.

Drone Racing

VR has already enabled a new form of spectator sport: drone racing. Players race unmanned drones at speeds up to 200 mph. The devices zoom over, around and through obstacles set up in athletic stadiums and shopping malls.

Human pilots sitting safely on the ground use remote controls and HMDs to pilot the drones. The VR software gives them a first-person view (FPV). For the operators, it feels as if they are sitting atop their drones, whizzing through obstacles while navigating dangerously close to competitors.

Will this become the equivalent of Formula One racing for Millennials and Minecrafters? It is too soon to tell, but in due time, attendees will be able to enjoy headsets that give them the same adrenaline-pumping experience as the operators feel through FPVs.

Crashes are far more frequent in drone racing than in race car competition. When they do occur, the debris is comprised of splintered plastic, devoid of the blood and bone that results from many Formula One crashes.

While drone racing is not yet a ready-for-prime-time sport, there is a grassroots movement gaining in interest and investment. Steve Ross, owner of the Miami Dolphins, has ponied up $1 million for hosting drone races at Sun Life Stadium, home of his football team.

Drone racing may or may not make it to the level of a major sport. We include it here because it shows how VR is going to create new destination activities that will be enjoyed in ways that are different from anything we have today.

Social VR

As early social media champions, we could not help but notice that most of the VR apps we were seeing involved the simultaneous participation of just a few people, usually only one or two at a time. Israel worried that VR may be entertaining, but no more social than watching a movie in a dark theater, where you may be aware of people around you and share in laughter and applause, but are essentially having a solo experience.

Scoble knew better, so he brought his slower-adopting co-author to AltSpaceVR where he met Eric Romo, founder and CEO, and Bruce Wooden, head of development and community relations. Then Israel understood social VR's massive potential.

Wooden served as his guide. In his avatar, he appeared entirely different from in real life. Israel used a high-end Vive whose controllers are adept at picking up and moving items. Wooden's avatar taught Israel to pick up a sword for a virtual duel in a medieval tavern. While Wooden was still giving friendly instructions, Israel lunged forward and slashed Wooden's avatar to slivers. Israel howled with laughter while Wooden's avatar reassembled.

The tour continued, with Wooden's resurrected avatar escorting Israel through a variety of fun and immersive activities. Occasionally, another avatar would wander onto the VR set as well, for no apparent reason.

When it was over, and Israel removed his headset, he had the strange sensation that he and Wooden had become old friends, even though Wooden had appeared in the VR world as an entirely different character. Israel felt a compulsion to hug his host; It was like meeting an old friend for the first time.

We dwell on this because it shows an entirely new level of social media's ability to create friendships between total strangers in VR. On Facebook, friendships form over several encounters. Perhaps it takes months, but in AltSpace it had happened in about 20 minutes.

This was just one aspect of the potential of social VR as Romo described it to us. Since coming out of beta just a few months earlier, the site has hosted thousands of visitors in nearly 150 countries. People are staying for an average of 40 minutes. It is not uncommon for gamers to stay for six-hour stints. Wooden once spent nine hours immersed in the site: "After a while, the brain accepts the virtual space as real space and you start thinking that the avatars you encounter are real people. They evoke real emotions."

One time Romo and Wooden were virtually meeting when Wooden's avatar looked away. Romo became annoyed that he was being ignored—as he would have had they both been in the same room.

The company was still in its early phases, still working out its monetization plans. Romo said that its ideas are falling into two groups: experiences and events.

Virtual events have some advantages over real events: Virtual attendance space is unlimited, so a big-name rock group could perform on AltSpace and sell tickets to fans worldwide. In addition to admission, it can take in sponsorship dollars just like NFL teams. It can sell virtual souvenirs. We forgot to ask them about virtual beers.

Experiences would be sold to groups that join to do something together, perhaps make music or have virtual swordfights like the one in which Israel took out Wooden. The experience could be training, such as teaching new casino dealer the finer points of blackjack or how to juggle.

While VR started early in 2016 in forms that provided individual experiences, the year has increasingly demonstrated VR's enormous social potential.

Mark Zuckerberg called it the most social technology he knows. And in October 2016, just as we were wrapping up this book for publication, Oculus announced a new, fully tracked wireless headset in the works and let Oculus Connect conference attendees play with the prototype.

The wireless headsets are a significant step in the direction of truly mobile devices and are designed for socialization and game playing by groups.

Price and availability were not mentioned, but attendees said it sounded very much as if the new devices will be out for Christmas 2016.

Big Numbers. Big Future

When you look at the numbers associated with the games we talked about in the previous chapters and those we have discussed here, you need to step back and think very, very big.

According to *Business Insider*, VR headsets alone will grow from a $37 million dollar industry in 2015 to $2.8 billion in 2020—growing by a factor of 75. Goldman Sachs predicts revenue from all categories of VR including software will reach $110 billion by 2020, making the category bigger than the TV industry in its first five years.

We are futurists, but not number-crunchers. All we know is that VR is going to get a whole lot bigger in a very short period of time.

Any way you measure, VR is going to be a major event. While it starts in games and entertainment, as we'll describe, it will have an even bigger impact in retail, the enterprise, healthcare and education.

VR is the first significant step on a long road that culminates when technology and people are no longer separated by screens, when reality and computer-generated images become so tightly integrated that you just can't tell one from the other.

There are two other separate but related technologies: augmented and mixed reality. Let's look at where they are starting and where they are heading.

+++++

CHAPTER 4

Standing Upright

"Look forward to the future and look forward to the unknown."

—Angela Merkel, prime minister

In the evolution from mobile technology into the Fourth Transformation, we are just now crawling out of the swamp. We have reached the developmental phase where the world sees the promises of AR and VR. But these are merely early precursors to what will compel people to move from the mobile devices of the third transformation to walking fully upright with head-mounted devices designed and priced for everyday people.

The VR that we have talked about so far has already demonstrated the transformational capabilities of virtual reality, at least in games and entertainment.

But in the great transformation we envision, they are just the earliest forms, the evolution from things that swim into a more amphibious state, in which many important creations dwell partly in the waters they are departing. As they evolve onto the land they will slither and then crawl; there will come a point where they will walk stooped over with arms dangling.

Ultimately, this great migration will deliver people and technology into the new Age of Spatial Computing, and then we will walk upright, boldly going beyond anywhere we have been.

Before we get to the point where shoppers go online or into tony boutiques to select competitively priced, chic smart glasses with designer logos, much must happen.

There are many technology barriers to clear before these new head-worn devices contain all that is needed. Their current evolution is developing in two directions.

First is the continuation of the trusty smartphone that goes where we go today. It is acquiring new AR functionality in the form of valuable or entertaining new apps and devices that do what could not previously be done with a handset. Because the phone is still evolving as we write in 2016, it is difficult to picture life without it or with phones as a secondary accessory.

Five years from now, we see a different story. The innovation will have moved to headsets; people who have them will be spending more minutes on headsets and fewer on their old handsets.

Ten years out almost all the innovation will be on the headsets, and they will become the center of digital life.

Headsets keep exceeding expectations and innovations are coming faster than customers expected; and, as we heard from Vive, Meta and HoloLens, customers are coming faster than the developers expected.

No one saw a pent-up demand when headsets first appeared at the January 2016 CES show. But they have evolved quickly, and millions of them are in use as we write ten months later. We believe that this will prove to be the dominant evolutionary strain, the one that will accompany humans as they walk upright into the coming Age of Spatial Computing.

Even so, as we write, the most explosive action in AR is not on an expensive headset but in a free mobile phone app. Even Mark Zuckerberg, whose company invested $2 billion for Oculus Rift VR headsets, has declared that AR will go mainstream on phones before glasses. He's right.

So let's start with what is today's best known AR product.

See Pokemon Go

Nintendo became a global video game powerhouse in 1996 when it introduced Pokemon for its Game Boy console. The game was the most popular in its category, featuring adorable cartoonish animals that players hunted as trophies. Highly addictive and supposedly for kids, the game endured for nearly a decade before enthusiasm atrophied as it failed to improve as technology and competition overtook it.

Pokemon was pretty much forgotten by the time Nintendo teamed up with Google to form Niantic Labs, the mobile gaming company that on July 7, 2016, launched Pokemon Go in the U.S., Australia and New Zealand.

By the end of that day, it was the world's most downloaded app. In four days, it hit 7.5 million and by month's end, it had been downloaded over 75 million times. It was also immediately among the stickiest of all mobile apps, being played an average of 43 minutes daily, more than Instagram, WhatsApp or Snapchat.

The essential game hadn't changed much. What had changed a lot was the technology. Pokemon Go brought three innovations:

1. You play it while walking around.
2. You see Pokemon creatures, or "trophies," on top of the real world in augmented reality.
3. Pokemon uses phone sensors to control the playing surface.

Players start off by walking around looking at a map. They click when they see a character and that switches them into AR mode, where the trick is to bag trophies by beaning them with red-and-white virtual balls to score points.

When players run out of the balls, they must visit Pokestops, real places of interest in the player's neighborhood where they stock up on items that allow them to advance in the game. To obtain the balls, they use PokeCoins, which are a form of virtual cash that you acquire with real money charged to your credit card.

And therein lies a very clever monetization model.

The folks at Niantic aren't yet saying, but we see all sorts of additional possibilities. Brands could pay to have their logos attached to Pokemon trophies. When you bag one, the brand could award some little prize. PokeStops could start moving into malls, shops and theaters, where people may discover offers near their trophies.

As of August, Pokemon Go was indisputably the top tech story of the year, and it has been a very newsworthy year.

However, there remains a debate as to whether Pokemon Go is something enduring or just a fad, a modern variation of the hula hoop or pet rock. If it follows the history of the earlier version of the same game, Pokemon Go could end up being called Pokemon Gone.

Frankly, we don't care.

What matters to us is that Pokemon shows how compelling AR—in its simplest form—can be to everyday people. This simple little game went mainstream on its first day and remained there for more than six weeks.

Because of this, more than 100 million people have experienced AR that may otherwise not have joined the ranks. This doesn't mean that they are about to toss their phones and opt for headsets. It does mean that the AR phenomenon has been further demystified. Over 100 million people now know a little more about AR and will be a little more inclined to try it on a headset in the hope of having an enhanced experience.

And this is a key point of our evolutionary metaphor. Handsets make you appreciate the AR experience; headsets make you love it. As the devices themselves evolve, more and more people will opt for having headsets. In millions of cases, phones and head-mounted devices work together and will continue to do so for at least five more years.

But as today's tethered, large and slightly clumsy headsets move toward being self-contained, fashionable smart glasses, they will take over the functionality of today's smartphones and in many, many cases, the user experience will be a lot better.

Let's look at another application you have probably heard about, one that has many millions more users, most of them in the newest and sweetest spot on marketing demographic target lists.

Pinsnapping

Snapchat introduced AR on mobile phones in 2015 as part of its successful strategy to become the social platform of choice for youth and young adults.

It's a strategy that has worked well. Since the startup was ridiculed for spurning Facebook's $3 billion acquisition offer when its revenue was near zero, its valuation has grown to $20 billion.

It has overtaken Facebook in popularity with Minecrafters and Millennials. About 60% of US smartphone users between the ages of 13 and 34 are regular Snapchat users and, in 2016, it is the fastest growing social network.

There are many reasons for this success, including its use of video and mobile technologies as well the way it creates a sense of urgency and currency by having video clips disappear 24 hours after they post.

Snapchat latched onto a successful monetization tactic with *Lenses*, a feature which allows Snapchatters to post photos of themselves inside the heads of AR fish, or with hearts for eyes, or—Scoble's favorite—barfing rainbows as their eyes pop out in cartoon fashion.

Lenses expose young users to AR in an easy and light-hearted way. For example, while watching a friend's video post, you might see an AR version of the White Rabbit, looking at his watch, dart across your phone screen, revealing to you that the sender is in a hurry.

AR hares and rainbows lack the sophistication and elegance that you might enjoy on, say, an HTC Vive headset. But the user's cost is near zero. Snapchat is using a modern variation of the classic television sponsorship model, and brands like Coke, Red Bull, Disney and Taco Bell are jumping in. Marketers can focus on a younger demographic at a particular point in time and in a narrow and specific location.

This exemplifies *Pinpoint Marketing*, a technique that we describe in three earlier books: the ability for brands to make offers to people based on their location, time of day, personal profiles and buying patterns. In our previous writing, we talked more about how we thought marketing *should be* than how it actually is.

Now marketers seem more enlightened to the value of Pinpoint Marketing. Snapchat is the first company to prosper with its own take on this strategy, which we call *pinsnapping*.

Let's look at a few examples.

Brian Fanzo consults for big brands such as IBM, Deloitte and SAP, sharing expertise on marketing to Millennials. He told us how his clients could use Snapchat's *geofilters* to send event-related offers just to Snapchat users attending a college basketball game or rock concert.

Pinsnapping lets big brands get local and personal so they can customize offers to millions of people attending thousands of events—a few people at a time. Instead of mass marketing, the company has developed a form of *mass micro marketing* and early results show great promise.

Marketing maestro Gary Vaynerchuk, who wrote our Foreword, told *Business Insider,* "Snapchat is the best marketing tool you can use right now," and he demonstrated how with a little experiment of his own at SXSW 2016.

During the Austin-based festival, he set up a table on a different sidewalk on each day of the festival, using a customized Snapchat geofilter at each. He invited attendees nearby to post videos on Snapchat on why they wanted to meet him.

In the course of the week, thousands of Snapchatting Millennials posted clips, which they collectively shared with tens of thousands of friends. Each day, Vaynerchuk picked one winner who then met up with Vaynerchuk to receive the prize: posing for yet another Snapchat video with Vaynerchuk. The reward for promoting him was to promote him some more.

This is something new that we would call *Celebrity Pinpoint Marketing,* and we are sure smart marketers will find all sorts of ways to use this to promote luminaries, events and specific items on a store shelf.

Like Pokemon Go, Snapchat is providing opportunities to marketers who understand the wisdom of adding contextual factors such as time and place. This way they can simultaneously reduce costs and improve response while pissing off far fewer people by filtering out shoppers who don't want irrelevant marketing messages.

Snapchat is going through its own evolution from a mobile social network into what looks like a mobile social AR company. In September 2016, it launched a pair of 3D video-enabled sunglasses called Spectacles for $130. The devices use Bluetooth or Wi-Fi to transfer videos of 10 seconds or less directly to the Snapchat phone app.

The glasses have the same field of view as the human eye, and this will be a factor when the glasses become AR devices, which we assume will be soon. They are based on technology acquired when Snapchat bought Vergence Labs, which, prior to the acquisition, made a little 3D camera you can attach to regular eyeglasses.

The Spectacles product was about to ship as we were wrapping up this book. If the first version does not have 3D capability, we assume there will soon be a future version that will.

We see this as a product that will rapidly emerge, becoming lower in price and increasing in functionality as well as in outrageously hip styles.

A logical companion will come from Snapchat's acquisition of Obvious Engineering, which will enable Snapchatters to take 3D selfies.

Hinting further at the company's evolution, Snapchat changed its company name to Snap, Inc., and declared that it was now a camera company. We think it would be more inclusive to say it is a mobile, social camera company, with significant and enthusiastic support from Millennials and older Minecrafters.

Snap currently uses the most primitive forms of augmented reality. Spectacles show the novelty and creativity of AR, but fail to show the full potential of 3D capabilities that they could by employing a gyroscope to understand the direction a user is moving in and an accelerometer that measures velocity of motion. They also do not provide stereoscopic sound, which is part of the AR headset experience.

This stripped-downed version is affordable, however, and unlike higher-end headsets, it is as mobile as a smartphone. Like Pokemon Go, the simplicity and fun of the product will make it wildly popular, making millions more people enthusiastic about AR experiences.

Snapchat becoming Snap is indicative of the evolution upon which this book is based. When people use Snapchat, they walk with head down and hands occupied in the posture of the cave dwellers we talked about in the previous chapter. With Snap Spectacles, the posture becomes heads up and hands free. The phone is still necessary, but over time, the function of the social networking app will be swallowed by the headset.

That is the natural progression.

Head up and Hands Free

As far as we could determine, the people who are pioneering the Fourth Transformation are unanimous in believing that the future of AR is in mixed reality. Smart glasses that integrate reality and computer-generated images so tightly that you cannot tell the difference between them are the main event in terms of products that will drive the Fourth Transformation.

Why? Because the best way to experience AR is in a headset. It may surprise you to know that many of the world's largest industrial operations have tried and tested this kind of AR for a very long time, far before the term *AR* was used in the context of end users.

The concept of AR glasses has been around since the 1960s, when heavy manufacturing workers and field workers started using them. We'll tell you more about what is going with workers' use of AR in Chapter 8. We mention it here because it provides additional evidence that this technology will be a fundamental force driving the Fourth Transformation.

Founded in 1999, Osterhout Design Group (ODG) is the grand-daddy of AR head-mounted devices. Ralph Osterhout had previously designed night-vision goggles for the military and heads-up displays for scuba divers before founding ODG to serve military partners. ODG still works with the military but has expanded into industrial, energy, automotive and agricultural uses and is a favorite hardware device for AR software developers.

In 2016, it launched the ODG R-8, the eighth revision of its headset and the third using 3D technology. We found it to be a highly refined product. We were impressed with ODG's two tiny, stereoscopic screens that provided an impressively wide field of view. Nima Shams, VP of Headworn, told us the screens were equivalent to watching a cinema-quality movie on a 100-inch-wide TV screen six feet in front of you.

Among ODG's partners is BMW, which customizes the headset with software for Mini drivers so they can enjoy the safety of heads up dashboard information. Both Stanford Medical Center and Johns Hopkins University use ODG AR eyewear to restore vision to patients who are visually impaired due to macular degeneration, the leading cause of blindness.

As AR becomes more popular, ODG faces new players. Silicon Valley-based Atheer Air was the newest kid on the AR headset block, launching in the summer of 2016. Its competitive advantage is that is an open system with Wi-Fi, Bluetooth and 4G LTE cellular roaming capabilities. Users can communicate with each other by 3D gestures and through directional voice interaction.

Atheer Air targets *"deskless professionals,"* a market to which ODG has not paid much attention.

But wait, there's more—a lot more.

There are at least 10 AR headset brands today, and we'd be surprised if that number didn't double in the coming years. We see AR having increasing value in industrial and niche environments, where appearance is not an issue and the objective is for employees to have hands-free access to relevant data suitable for repairs, field work and remote surgeries, and to provide drivers of cars, boats, trains and jets with safer access to dashboard data.

A market with lots of competitors is good for customers. Competition drives innovation up and prices down.

Just a Start

This has been a chapter about little steps, steps that are driving an imminent massive change in just about everything.

To extend our evolutionary metaphor just a little bit further, it took millions of years for humans to evolve from swamp crawling to upright, hands-free modern Homo sapiens.

Now it is time to look at what happens as technology evolves rapidly on the evolutionary path to the coming Age of Spatial Computing. Let's move on to that MR main event we mentioned.

+++++

CHAPTER 5

The Main Event

"Truth or illusion, George; you don't know the difference."

—Edward Albee, absurdist

I n our last chapter, we told you that mixed reality was the main event. Yet, as we write, we have not yet heard of a single example of someone wearing an AR headset into a tavern, a workplace or a shopping mall.

So why write about this now?

Because things are happening very fast, and companies—particularly big ones—like to dip their toes into new technologies before plunging in.

Millions of people have already adopted VR and AR technologies and are spending more and more time in them—and they are merely the opening acts.

The first mixed reality headsets have already arrived, and there are more coming. They are not quite ready for consumer use: Each headset costs as much as $3,000, their current designs would likely face the same unwelcome reception that Google Glass did four years ago, and the software that is needed for people to do their work and communicate has not quite arrived—although some may be available by the time you read this.

So let's talk about what's here already, and then we'll talk about what the current challenges are and why we see them more as little speed bumps rather than great barriers.

David vs Goliath

Every digital transformation has started with new hardware, and the hardware that has arrived, or soon will, has generated most of the excitement. That's what may have motivated you to read this book.

While a transformation may start with hardware, the evolution from the early tech enthusiasts into the mainstream requires software. And as you saw in the first four chapters, there is already a great deal happening in VR software and experiences.

But let's look at the headsets that are so much in the news and are generating so much enthusiasm and speculation.

Back-to-Back

Microsoft HoloLens and Meta, a Silicon Valley startup, launched the first two MR headsets back-to-back as the lead presentations at the prestigious TED conference n March 2016. Both caused big stirs.

While the two demos showed many different attributes, they both chose the same app for their compelling conclusions. They showed how two people in separate locations could actually talk to each other in real time. In previous transformations, this was called a phone conversation and really isn't that big of an event. But these conversations were closer to the Star Trek versions—in fact, they were better.

When Meron Gribetz, Meta CEO and co-founder, used the new Meta 2 to call up a colleague, his friend appeared live on the stage as a hologram. The two exchanged a precise fist bump that showed how real and virtual hands could sense and respond to each other using MR.

HoloLens took it a step further. Creator Alex Kipman chatted with a NASA official who was in a hotel room across the street: But to attendees and worldwide livestream viewers, the NASA guy appeared to be on Mars. The 3D background was built on data collected from Rover's visit to the Red Planet.

B2B Partners

Microsoft, a company that probably enjoys as many long-standing corporate partnerships as any, had announced deals with Trimble Architecture, Case Western Reserve University, Volvo, Saab, Audi, Volkswagen, Levi's, Lowe's, Unity, Autodesk, and Disney. Each of these companies seems likely to have consumer strategies in mind.

But Microsoft is also making first forays into reaching consumers through its other platforms including Xbox consoles, where MR games such as an MR Minecraft are in broad retail distribution, and Skype, where the headsets presumably will allow people to have the sort of conversations that they demonstrated at TED.

Chris Capossela, Microsoft CMO, declared in April 2016, two months after HoloLens started shipping, "We totally underestimated the commercial interest in this thing," and Microsoft is scrambling to catch up on backlogged products—far from the worst problems a global powerhouse can face.

Soren Harner, Meta's chief product officer, also told us that in the first two months following TED, Meta 2 orders exceeded all orders the company had received in the 18 months that the Meta 1 was its flagship product. He said Meta was hottest in seven categories: medical, automotive, energy, manufacturing, aerospace, defense and finance. The company also revealed a deal with a major theme park that wants to give visitors the experience of wilder rides.

The startup has raised $50 million from China's Lenovo, the world's largest personal computer maker; Tencent, China's largest social network; and Comcast, the media giant. All three investors have obvious and extensive access to consumer markets.

In June, Lenovo announced that Meta would be part of its global strategy to become "a lot more than just a computer maker," according to Yang Yuanqing, Lenovo's CEO.

These early successes add to the increasing stack of evidence that MR headsets such as these will start to attract customers when price and design issues are inevitably resolved.

Containment and Software

Both companies would readily agree that neither product is ready for mass consumer adoption just yet. HoloLens headsets cost $3,000 each and have a limited field of view that critics have likened to watching HDTV through a mail slot. Worse, the Meta 2 is still tethered to a computer, an even greater drawback.

But these are not great obstacles to reaching consumer markets; they seem to us to be mere bumps on the road ahead, the sort of problems that Moore's Law continues to resolve over time.

There are two bigger issues:

1. **Self-containment.** The CPU, GPU (graphics processing unit), Wi-Fi, power, wiring, sensors, cameras, 3D screens, stereoscopic sounds and other componentry all need to be contained in a single, hands-free wearable device that is independent of the phone it will eventually replace.

2. **Software.** We are amazed at how far software has come since the ill-fated debut of Google Glass. We'll tell you more about it in this chapter and those that follow. But a great deal needs to happen in the next few years, including the emergence of productivity and communications software.

    Even the games and entertainment we've talked about so far need refinement. VR needs to be adapted into a mode that can be used in other settings to drive cars and walk about. What people are loving today with Pokemon Go and Snapchat will look like cave drawings compared with what MR glasses will be able to show you.

We have high confidence that these two issues will be resolved in the next two to five years. Why? Because there are other hardware players lurking, and some of the world's most creative people are now becoming software developers in these spaces.

Meanwhile, we are seeing advances in software that are literally like nothing anyone has ever seen, because developers are working on technology that has never existed.

Software Studios

The way software is being developed now resembles the way movies are made. Developers' workplaces are increasingly called *studios*. The people designing software are resembling movie makers and animators more and more. This seems fitting, when you consider that this software will deliver the Visual Web that we described in Chapter 1.

Up in Seattle, there's a design studio called Loook.io. They create mixed reality properties for headset makers. Today, their biggest client is HoloLens. Scoble visited them in the summer of 2016. Here's how he describes it:

> You walk into their office, and there is no office. The only things that are real are the people who work there and a Bluetooth keyboard, with which they click here and there and weird and cool things happen:
>
> Someone clicks on the keyboard, and a window suddenly appears on a bare wall; another click, and zombies start to climb through it. Then he clicks on a virtual button hovering in midair to start a Skype call to a friend who appears in the room as a hologram.
>
> Another click, and five huge computer screens hover just above us. Those screens provide the team with all the information and tools they need to do their work.
>
> These virtual monitors are world changers. The Fourth Transformation computer is virtual and will save offices a great deal of money and real estate, although it bodes poorly for monitor makers: When your interface is the world about you, monitors are just another item to fold into the virtual properties like the ones I saw at Loook.

Everywhere Scoble looked, he saw weird and useful stuff that will be in homes and stores, factories and medical facilities in more and more places in the next five years.

Loook is not alone. MR studios are forming all over the world, attracting many of the world's most talented and creative designers. Los Angeles has almost as many 3D design studios as medical marijuana parlors.

MR Technology

As we've stated, mixed reality combines the best aspects of VR and AR, integrated so tightly that you cannot discern the difference between the two. Using haptic sensors, it even gives MR headset users a sense of touch and temperature.

Here are some of the effects that explain the magic of this experience:

- **It sucks light from air.** Optical componentry blacks out the light in front of you, replacing what is actually there with computer-generated images. That's how in Magic Leap's demo, a whale jumps out of the floor.
- **It watches you.** Sensors in your lenses watch where you look. So when you look at a Coke can on a store shelf, 3D images jump in front of your eyes, giving you a special offer or telling you about the ingredients.
- **It learns about you.** Using artificial intelligence, your device sees what you look at and how your eye reacts, so it knows what you like or what makes you laugh. It knows when you are bored or drunk. It knows what you probably want based on where you are and where you are looking. In our experience, this is both valuable and freaky.
- **It augments audio.** Stereoscopic sound creates an audio that is better than real. You can use earbuds at a concert and enjoy the sensation that the instruments are surrounding you.

- **The world is your interface.** In MR, the barrier of a screen is eliminated, and you become immersed in the technology. Yes, you'll know these items that you see are fake, but after wearing a headset for a few minutes, your mind will accept them as real. This is spatial computing, the ultimate destination of the Fourth Transformation.
- **It maps the world in 3D.** Sensors on your MR glasses create 3D maps of everything you see. They map that table and floor where you are sitting. Wherever you look, what you see gets mapped. This mapping is essential to creating a new spatial computing science of visually classifying objects and eliminating the need to use words in a particular human language to find what you want online.
- **You can touch and move things.** Anything mapped can be manipulated, and menus can be laid on top of it. This changes how you interact with any object connected to the IoT.
- **You can see the data.** Your glasses are also connected to the IoT, so any time you encounter another IoT-connected object you will be able to read data from it to, for example, adjust a thermostat, buy an object in a store window or see the bio of the person in front of you at a conference based on data embedded in her badge.

Most people will know when a device is MR just by looking through it. But from a business perspective—or even just as users—we think it is important to understand just what is going on within technologies like HoloLens and Meta 2.

Giants in the Shadows

There are two other players that we expect to enter the consumer MR market and become formidable competitors. As with Microsoft and Meta, one is a tech industry leader and the other is a startup with no track record at all in the marketplace.

The startup is Magic Leap, a company that has generated excitement. The Florida-based company has raised a record $1.3 billion from a group headed by Google and Alibaba. As we write this, it has no finished product, no customers and no announced ship date—but those who have seen and tried the product under non-disclosure seem unable to praise it enough.

For example, Ted Schilowitz, resident futurist at 20th Century Fox, told us that it was the "first trillion-dollar idea." That's a pretty big idea: about seven times what it cost, in today's dollars, to put someone on the moon and then bring him back.

The other player is Apple Computer, which has spent billions acquiring companies and filing patents that indicate it will play big in the MR device market. On any given day, Apple is likely to be in the top three most valuable companies on Earth. It tends to enter markets once they are established and to dominate the high end.

If we are to call this another David versus Goliath matchup, Magic Leap is one of the biggest, most promising Davids ever. Let's take a look at them first.

From what we have gathered through multiple sources, Magic Leap uses a different—and superior—system for MR compared with what HoloLens and Meta are doing.

In simplest terms, the two existing products watch where the eye is looking and understand what is seen by using depth sensor cameras, gyroscopes and accelerometers. They then create point clouds and then build virtual objects on point clouds.

That system is damned good. It lets you see computer-generated images sitting on top of a real objects and to touch and manipulate those objects.

But the elite few who have seen Magic Leap under NDA tell us we ain't seen nothing yet. Magic Leap creates a visual effect in which those wearing the devices can barely tell what is real and what is not, because the lens optics are vastly superior to those contained in earlier headsets.

Magic Leap devices do not look very different from the glasses everyday people wear today, but they contain tiny, nanoscopic, outwardly reflecting mirrors. Instead of projecting images on top of what is there, the mirrors black out the view and replace it with virtual images, creating a far sharper image.

Shortly before our deadline, Jono MacDougall posted an in-depth article at *UploadVR*, where Scoble is entrepreneur in residence. MacDougall had gone after the story of Magic Leap by digging into patent records, job applications and company resumes.

According to MacDougall, the headset is just slightly larger than optical glasses and not much heavier. To accomplish what others have not yet done, Magic Leap reduced the technology contained in the frames by moving the central and graphical processing units, power, Wi-Fi, Bluetooth, RAM and the critical laser projection system into a pocket device that resembles a screenless smartphone. A USB cable connects it to the headset.

The outward-facing camera was also moved to the peripheral component, partly to avoid the privacy issue related to hidden cameras.

MacDougall concludes that the smart device will produce a level of realism "beyond what we have seen so far from other similar devices."

Such a device would leapfrog the *current* HoloLens and Meta 2 devices significantly, taking a great leap toward the one Zuck imagined. It would only be a matter of time before Moore's Law would allow reduction of size and increase of power in the components housed in the tethered pocket device.

But we stress *current* because we don't know when HoloLens will actually bring a product to market, and we don't know how much the two incumbent products will have improved by that time. There is a big difference in the impact of a product depending on whether it arrives in 2017, 2020 or 2022.

Our sources tell us that Magic Leap will have developer preview devices in 2017, but at the end of the day, we'll just have to wait and see.

There is also the possibility that the product, as is being described, may never come to market. But we believe it will.

The same goes for that other giant in the shadows.

Charisma and Arrogance

The fifth anniversary of Steve Jobs' death was observed in October 2016. The tech sector, which tends to be long on vision and short on memory, still feels his influence.

Jobs envisioned, oversaw and introduced more game-changing hardware than anyone before or after him. This includes, of course, the Macintosh, iPhone and iPad. He personally launched these and other significant products at industry events, displaying his unique combination of charisma and arrogance.

His strategy was consistent. Apple was never first to market. He let others take the risks and learn the lesson of tech pioneering. Then, after a few years, after market viability was established, he would take the stage and introduce Apple's late entry, very often declaring that anything that preceded it to market "was just crap."

And the market consistently responded by agreeing with Jobs, that Apple products were more elegant, more expensive and worth the money because compared with them, the other stuff just wasn't as good.

Since Jobs' death, there has been no disruptively revolutionary hardware introduced by Apple or anyone else—until mixed reality headsets came along.

The Cupertino giant remains as tight-lipped under its new CEO Tim Cook as it was under Jobs. No major company in technology has a better track record of keeping secrets.

It also keeps cash reserves of over $200 billion, so the fact that it has tossed out a few billion dollars to buy up over 15 tech-rich startups since 2012 impacts its wealth about as much as yours is impacted when you stock up with an extra loaf of bread.

Apple's acquisitions include makers of sensor chips and cameras, indoor and outdoor mapping, 3D and 360-degree cameras, facial recognition and alteration software, AR software, motion capture and depth sensing technology, machine learning and data compression. All of these could be used to build a next-generation MR device, even before the current generation of these devices plays out.

Apple has more cash reserves than the United Kingdom. It has amassed this fortune primarily from computers and more recently smartphones. Apple's returns in those two categories will diminish. So, like Google, it explores new technologies of the near future such as augmented cars and enhanced reality. Or so we believe; the company holds its product plans so close to its vest that they might as well be tattoos.

We know even less about what Apple is up to than we know about Magic Leap. If it were close to launching a headset, we would probably find out through the same type of searches that MacDougall used to project what Magic Leap is up to, so we are guessing its product is several years away.

We doubt that Tim Cook will ever be either as arrogant or charismatic as his predecessor. But we take him as a shrewd long-term player who understands that Apple's play in this new arena has bet-the-company implications.

We are entering a period where great hardware makers of yore understand that if they do what they have always done, they will not survive or, at best, will end up as irrelevant as Sears stores or Maytag repairmen.

Meanwhile, the folks at Meta and HoloLens keep on refining product, getting as far out on the runway as possible before the giants emerge from the shadows. The teams at Magic Leap and Apple continue to develop what they hope will make great leaps forward into the Fourth Transformation.

Who will the winners be? All of us, because digital technology will serve us as consumers and workers far better than most of us ever imagined.

As for the headset makers themselves, to be honest, it doesn't matter who the winners are. While it is interesting to watch such a grand competition, what matters to us is that four brilliant teams are laboring to develop and refine products as fast as possible, and that countless developers are creating things beyond what anyone has ever seen before. As in the recent past, demand from Millennials and Minecrafters will drive what will happen in the near future.

The Fourth Transformation cannot be stopped.

But, as the late Steve Jobs used to say, "There's one more thing."

When you put on your smart glasses in the near future, how will you communicate what you want to do?

We weren't sure about this until we stumbled upon Eyefluence and found a really good answer.

+++++

CHAPTER 6
The Missing Link

Gerund is a term that refers to words ending in *-ing*. It was easy for us to find gerunds that summarized the interfaces in the first three transformations: *typing, clicking* and *touching*.

But it took us a while to figure out our gerund for the Fourth Transformation. We had heard all sorts of ideas for how people would interact when wearing headsets. They included *tapping, winking, blinking, tracking, talking* and *gesturing*.

Two of these have some staying power in our minds: Gesturing and talking will be used in many cases: But more than anything else, we will be *interacting*. And unlike the situation we described in the previous chapter, in this chapter we find only one company capable of making that happen.

The company is Eyefluence, and it is the missing link that will let headset users walk upright in ways that will change work and life at least as much as the iPhone, Mac and DOS did.

At about the time that Google Glass with all its tapping and talking commands began floundering, in 2013, two serial entrepreneurs with solid track records, Jim Marggraff and David Stiehr, acquired some *eye-tracking* software technology

This, in itself was no big deal: eye tracking has been around for over 130 years. It came to computers in the 1980s when the psychologists Marcel Just and Patricia Carpenter theorized brains process what they see as fast as the eye sees it.

Computerized eye tracking has valuable uses today in psychology, psycholinguistics and other health-related fields. It enables quadriplegics to manipulate objects on screens by nodding and blinking. Stephen Hawking's speech synthesis system uses eye tracking to help translate his thoughts into verbal communications.

In 2016, eye tracking found its way into spatial computing in the form of Fove, a VR headset that has garnered a fair amount of media attention.

But, according to Marggraff, Eyefluence builds upon an eye tracking foundation to create something new and superior that it calls *Eye Interaction*. Instead of just watching a user's eye, and taking cues from winks, blinks, nods or taps, the technology understands user intent and then acts without gesture or voice cues.

Marggraff asserts that Eyefluence is the only developer taking this approach. Having filed 30 patents to stake its claim, it has partnerships in various stages of development with "most major headset makers and many enterprises and brands," he told us.

We imagine its technology will be used in many—perhaps all—mixed reality glasses. Perhaps Magic Leap, Apple or some other player still lurking in the shadows is developing its own operating system to include a similar solution, but neither we nor Marggraff are aware of it.

This is technology that is better appreciated when used. We both have had demos separately. Scoble saw the software at SXSW and was blown away by it.

Israel looks more at business strategies and tends to be more skeptical about new technologies.

He visited Eyefluence in May of 2016 at the company's Milpitas, California, headquarters. He walked in carrying nagging doubts in his back-pack. Part of that stemmed from a comment Marggraff had said when they met briefly at SXSW: that Eyefluence would make digital glasses the one device that most people would use by the end of the next decade.

Israel had tried nearly all available major headsets. Each impressed him in one way or another, but none seemed to come close to devices that everyday people would place at the centers of their digital lives.

Could Israel ever write a book without a keyboard and monitor? Using mixed reality glasses to write a book simply seemed beyond the realm of the possible.

Accelerated Mole-Whacking

It took less than 15 minutes for Israel to be willing to swap his MacBook Air and iPhone for a new headset featuring Eyefluence software. The first two of those minutes were dedicated to Marggraff teaching Israel how to navigate with Eyefluence.

On the Home Page, he learned to effortlessly navigate among icons with his eyes. He booked a theoretical flight by interacting with a single icon. Then he saw how a doctor would call up medical records by looking at icons while simultaneously examining a patient.

Previously, Israel thought he had to go to technology to make things happen, but with Eyefluence, the technology came to him.

Prior to the demo, Marggraff had talked about how his Ph.D.-dominated team had spent years studying everything about the human eye. Israel had paid little attention: Nearly all entrepreneurs boast of team talents, and Silicon Valley probably has more Ph.D.s than Uber drivers.

Now, as he tested Eyefluence tech via an ODG headset, Israel quickly realized that as he watched virtual screens, the technology was watching him, was seeing where he looked and where his eye stopped. He intentionally moved his gaze away from where Marggraff was telling him to look, and the technology followed his eye and not his host's guiding voice: Eyefluence was getting to know Israel.

Next, Israel learned how and why the Eyefluence interface was faster and easier than anything he had previously encountered by playing Whac-a-Mole, a game introduced in its physical form in 1976. If you, like Israel, are among the few people on Earth unfamiliar with the game, know that the object is to clobber cute little rodents as they pop their heads out of the ground. The more moles you whack, the more points you get.

First, he played in an eye-tracking version. Every time a mole showed itself, Israel nodded and thus bopped the critter. As he got the hang of it he nodded and bopped at an accelerating rate. He thought he had done pretty well for a rookie.

Next, he tried Eyefluence's interaction software. Instead of nodding, he just moved his eyes naturally. This time, he whacked 40% more moles.

Next, Israel found himself looking through the headset at 40 screens surrounding him, covering 360-degrees horizontally and 180-degrees vertically—the full span of any headset environment. He could see what was on each screen. This was far different than the experience of having lots of tabs open on his home monitor. Israel could use his eyes to easily zoom into any screen, then scroll or manipulate with his eyes as he chose.

For the first time, Israel understood that this was what a typical computer environment will soon look like, and it did not seem to be even slightly freaky; it felt natural and productive.

Marggraff predicted that Eyefluence would be available for Israel the next time he wrote a book. It sounds like a good idea to us. We know lots of authors, and, like us, they find writing a book to be a messy and frustrating process. We take notes on multiple devices. We save tidbits in the form of links, *Post-it* notes or whatever is available. Israel has even jotted chapter ideas down on his kitchen chalkboard and names or links on the back of his hand.

That's the easy part. The challenge is to assemble all these disparate pieces into a cohesive chapter and then into a book where thousands of items fit snugly together like some sort of jigsaw puzzle.

Like most authors, Israel uses *Microsoft Word* for the assembly and production parts of the process. For Israel, it is an awkward and inefficient process and he has lost more than one vignette in this manner.

As he sat looking, Marggraff explained how he could cut and paste content from all 40 screens into just one, thus streamlining the assembly process, perhaps saving weeks of the most mundane parts of the book-writing process.

Eyefluence, it turned out, was developing a visual keyboard. In the near future, Israel would be able to write his entire book by just looking at keys, and it would be far faster than typing.

Paradigm-shifting moments are mentioned more often than they actually occur. But for Israel, this was one. He could think of nothing that would not be done better on an eye-interactive headset than on a mobile or desktop device—and he was eager to make the swap as soon as possible.

Eyefluential Agents

An important—and perhaps controversial—aspect of Eyefluence is its use of *intelligent agents,* a form of artificial intelligence that uses sensors and laser technology to detect changes, learn from them and then make autonomous decisions in response. This is how a sensor in a milk carton could generate an action. It would note the liquid is below a certain level, note the change and report it via the IoT to something like Amazon Echo or a set of smart glasses, which contain enough AI to either tell someone to buy milk or to order it autonomously, arranging for payment and delivery.

An Eyefluence-enabled headset uses sensors in the same way: to see your eyes move and in a millisecond or less make something happen in response. It can decide what you want and how it will fulfill your need.

The intelligent agent also remembers what it has learned and starts recognizing your patterns. It begins to anticipate that you usually need fresh milk every nine days or that the external temperature is below freezing, so it should tell your car to start and your garage door to open five minutes before you leave. If the weather is inclement, then it will alert you to leave early or alert others that you will show up late.

Intelligent agents watch your eyes. By watching your eyes, these agents know whether you are aroused or repulsed by what or who you are looking at.

If you are using a headset in a class or a work training program, your eyes will reveal to the intelligent agent when you are engaged and comprehending or when you are bored and distracted.

If you wear a mixed reality headset using agents such as *Eyefluence* provides, then the platform over time will probably know you better than any human in your life.

Marggraff said his agents were getting so good that they could demonstrate empathy; they have the ability to understand and share feelings. This is a quality generally perceived as the purview of humans and other higher-level life forms. One does not anticipate getting sympathy from a set of goggles.

We are sure this will freak a lot of people out.

But the benefits are pretty compelling. Eyefluence agents, according to Marggraff, can spot dyslexia, autism and other serious health-related issues in minutes.

This same empathetic quality will also reshape story-telling. The tale being told can adjust depending on what the viewer is feeling, and the characters in games will remember you from the last time you played; if you zapped one last time, you better be faster or have a new weapon or face getting zapped yourself this time.

If this is your first encounter with a character, it will quickly understand your intent because it is in fact looking into your eyes and understanding things about you, just as another human would.

Freaky or not, Eyefluence is part of something very big. It creates a missing link that makes your device of the near future faster, more natural and smarter than anything you have previously experienced.

On the last day that we worked on this book, Eyefluence became part of something bigger in another sort of way. Google announced on Oct. 30, 2016, that it would acquire the company for an undisclosed amount of cash and stock. This, of course, will greatly accelerate adoption of the eye interaction software.

While we don't believe that eye interaction will be the only way we will engage with technology in the Fourth Transformation—voice may be important, just as it is on phones—we do believe it will be the dominant method people use.

The repercussions in both retail and the enterprise are enormous. In fact, retail is about to change more in the next ten years than it has in the past 50. Let's take a look at that next.

+++++

PART 2

Business Changers

"Every generation needs a revolution."

—Thomas Jefferson, revolutionary thinker

CHAPTER 7
Ubiquitous Shopping

"It used to be that companies were built to last.
Now they are built to change."

—Lori Mitchell-Keller, SVP Retail, SAP

Over the coming decade, mixed reality technologies will change the way people shop. The boundaries between online and in-store will blur to the point where they will almost disappear. Shopping, like computing itself, will become ubiquitous.

The brands that realize this soonest will benefit the most; those that ignore it the longest will face the same destiny that local travel agents faced when airlines started selling tickets online.

Most major retail brands seem to be aware of the imminent transition and are already studying how and when to innovate. They find themselves maintaining a delicate balance. As Bridget Dolan, head of Sephora Innovation Labs explained, "we want to stay ahead of our customers in digital technology—but not too far."

But what is *not too far*? In retail, it means that before shoppers waltz into stores wearing MR headsets, they'll come in with handsets that have AR apps. This is already happening, thanks to Pokemon Go and Snapchat. We've even heard of a Pokemon Go player wearing a HoloLens in a store, perhaps the first such sighting of a new era.

MR and VR are about to reshape most aspects of retailing. They will be used in marketing and advertising, sometimes for better and perhaps sometimes for worse. But the two biggest changes will be in shopping locations, where changes have already begun, and shopper experiences, where the full impact will come in another two to three years when mixed reality devices become mobile.

If you are part of a big brand, you need to know about this now so you can understand how your customer relationships are about to change and so you begin to adjust course. If younger adults are important to your business, then you should move sooner rather than later.

You should also see these customers as an autonomous marketing channel, for they have greater influence on their peers than anything else. They do this primarily through social networks, but that influence is about to migrate into MR, as Snapchat is demonstrating.

The other reason you need to move fast is that the brands you serve or compete against are doing precisely that.

Coke, Condé Nast, Disney, the Golden State Warriors, Kellogg's, Lowe's, NASCAR, Nestlé, Nike, Pepsi, Viacom and Walmart have all brought VR and/or MR strategies to market already. Their efforts may be small and experimental now, but that's how big brands get started on big things: They get their toes wet, then go in a little deeper and if the testing shows warm waters, they take the full plunge.

We predict that the 2018 Christmas season will be a VR Christmas, not just because of headsets being purchased in stores, but because stores will be using VR to enhance customer experiences. After that, stores will see increasing numbers of shoppers in mobile versions of today's headsets, mostly Millennials and Minecrafters.

By 2020, most shoppers will be using AR and VR in personal devices. By 2025, shoppers will be overwhelmingly in headsets; only the elderly will still be using just phones.

Shoppers in smart glasses will look at products of interest and see product information and customer reviews. They will see selfie avatars of themselves wearing items in a choice of colors. When they see an item on a mannequin, a simple movement of the eyes will signal a wish to try an item on. The headsets will receive a code for a dressing room, allowing the customer to unlock the door. A human or robot clerk will deliver the right sizes to the customer's dressing room.

When you step out of the dressing room, a sales clerk will be signaled that you want human help. If not, you can make the purchase with Eye Interaction and just walk out of the store, as your smart glasses transmit proof of purchases to a sensor or security robot that you have paid.

Mixed reality technologies will spawn another important change to reality: Location will become less relevant. People will use smart glasses to shop when they see someone wearing shoes they like, zeroing in on a visible logo that your wearable device recognizes. Perhaps it will interact with a digital billboard in a train station to buy an item and have it delivered to your home or even delivered and waiting for you at the station where you disembark.

A little more than ten years out, passengers in autonomous cars will buy items with their eyes and screens embedded in smart windshields that record payment and arrange delivery via the IoT.

By 2025, smart glasses will be as ubiquitous as oxygen and many bigger brands are preparing for it.

But we get ahead of ourselves. Let's look at the biggest things that will exist by this Christmas or next.

Tango in the Aisles

We think Alphabet/Google has the most ambitious and diverse plans for the mixed technologies. We sense that it is not a unified companywide strategy, but many divisions of a very large and increasingly diverse operation, developing many products simultaneously with no clear master plan.

These products start at the low end with Google Cardboard, which unquestionably is the most distributed heads-up device. Google reported that 5 million had been shipped by January 2016, and we guess that number would be more than double by the time you read this.

Google has also started its own VR division, Google Daydream, which in October 2016 launched Daydream View, a new VR headset for $79, perhaps intended as a sturdier upgrade replacement for the nearly disposable, optically limited Cardboard or a challenger to Samsung's Gear VR.

Google's Daydream View is also limited, lacking the important navigation and location sensors that higher-end competitors have. But it is priced for low-end buyers, and it is a step into mobile VR because it is designed to go where users go, perhaps even to be worn all the time; still, it seems to us to be more of a portable device than a mobile one.

Meanwhile, other parts of Google/Alphabet are busy elsewhere.

The venture arm has bet heavily in the much-anticipated high-end Magic Leap MR glasses. Its autonomous cars are so far along that the company has put up a consumer-focused website to promote them. Like other autonomous cars, Google's will work with MR glasses, and both the car and the glasses will, of course, connect to the IoT to allow passengers to shop, socialize or be entertained as they move along the highways.

Google Maps has introduced a 3D AR component for teaching geographic information to children. The first module stars Verne, a friendly, animated, 500-foot-tall abominable snowman who frolics over the real Himalayas with his animated pet Yak.

In 2016, it introduced Tango. Tango is an AR system for mobile handsets, the most diverse and robust that we have seen by far. We spotlight it here because Tango shows how beneficial the new technologies can be in handset devices like the smartphones people use today.

When it introduced Tango in 2016, Google said it had development deals with hundreds of partners representing health, games, entertainment, training, education, construction, real estate and automotive.

Tango will drive changes in global retail, which is estimated to be a $30 trillion chunk of the global economy by 2025, according to McKinsey. At Lenovo Techworld in San Francisco in June 2016, we saw the device maker launch the Phab 2 Pro, the first Tango-enabled phone.

Johnny Lee, the driving force behind Tango, declared from the dais, "Every day we make thousands of little decisions to help us navigate through life. We walk, sit in chairs, make our way between the counter and sink on the way to our refrigerator. Human perceptions are fine-tuned in motion and navigation. But, so far, our tools—such as phones—have been unable to do so."

He very quickly built a point cloud on the stage, then converted it into a Fantasyland of psychedelic flowers and the sounds of fluttering songbirds that Phab 2 users would experience on their new 6.4-inch screens, which feature Dolby stereoscopic 360-degree immersive sound and full noise cancellation on the phone mike.

Then he showed how the same motion-tracking and depth-sensing technology will apply to daily experiences such as taking 3D measurements of a sofa in a store, then going home and projecting a precisely fitted image of that sofa into the living room; or taking photos of counters and faucets in 3D to preview them in a kitchen to be remodeled. He demonstrated the simple process of measuring a space and converting it into a schematic to bring to the lumber store for precise cuts of wood need for a new home cabinet.

We played a little with the Phab 2. It is sleek and elegant, longer and thinner than the iPhone 6 Plus, with a bigger screen. It was designed that way so that you can use Tango with one hand, an important feature for applications involving measurement.

The device contains a fisheye camera that enables motion tracking and a depth sensor that emits infrared signals that reflect back so that the device precisely understands the room's geometry. Working with the Tango software stack, the phone understands location without using GPS, Wi-Fi or beacons, all of which are less accurate.

According to Larry Yang, lead project manager, these features provide large-scale 3D pattern recognition while users are in motion, which current headsets can't yet accomplish.

At the partner kiosks, we measured a couch with ease and speed, then zapped virtual targets with Tango attached to a plastic gun. We watched live raptors as visitors to the New York Museum of Natural History will see them in front of reconstructed skeletons. The Tango Toybox featured several home entertainment selections including AR dominoes that could be played on real home furnishings and an AR puppy that was excessively cute.

All of these applications show the diverse ways that Tango phones can be used. Instead of dinosaurs in a museum, a toy department could have virtual critters greeting kids as they shop, or they could borrow a toy gun and shoot virtual aliens.

If Tango were just a software app, we think that it would be wildly successful. But, while we enjoyed the demos we explored, we wondered if they were enough for people to buy a new $500 phone. Might they prefer to keep their existing phone and enjoy similar experiences in, say, a Google Daydream headset selling for under $100?

We saw the greatest promise in partnerships and in two compelling use cases that may catapult Tango handsets forward with activities that you can't yet do with headsets: remodeling and mapping.

Saws, Drills and Phones

We talked with Kyle Nel, executive director of Lowe's Innovation Labs, after he presented at Techworld. Nel is a recognized thought leader on how big brands can adapt to disruptive technology.

Previously, the Labs created OSHbots for Lowe's subsidiary brand Orchard Supply Hardware (OSH). An OSHbot is a talking robot that greets shoppers as they enter selected OSH stores. The bots escort shoppers to their desired items and offer to get human assistance if requested. The AR is in the OSHbot's eyes, which are infrared sensors just like those in the Phab 2 phone and in all mixed reality headsets.

The soul of these robotic machines is artificial intelligence, and over time they will get smarter. At some point, they may actually sell products to customers, rather than turn them over to salespeople, because they will know every detail about every product in the store. Those robot eyes can scan bar codes and eventually take credit cards and complete transactions.

Lowe's Innovation Labs is also working on something called the HoloRoom. Similar—to the *Star Trek* Holodeck, HoloRooms will enable remodelers to see and immerse themselves in 3D models of the kitchens and bathrooms they plan to create. We visited a prototype in the Lowe's in Sunnyvale California. While the project when we saw it was disappointing in functionality, we loved the concept.

But here's where all this becomes important to Tango: Nel told us that Lowe's will be an authorized Phab 2 dealer when the phone ships. The home improvement superstore chain isn't diversifying to compete with local Verizon and AT&T stores, by any means. Instead, it will treat the new device as a power tool to make customer building and remodeling projects run faster, easier and more error free. In that context, a $500 investment makes sense to us—even if you never use the device to text or make a call.

Lowe's will equip sales associates with Phab 2s so they can use them to help shoppers. If a customer inquires about the phone, then there's an incremental sales opportunity.

In our view, home remodeling is a Tango killer app. It's a lot cheaper than a mistake in a remodeling project.

Interior Mapping

Google is unquestionably the world leader in desktop and mobile maps, but ironically, the technology is pretty useless the minute you step indoors. There are reasons for this.

Outdoors, map information such as mountains, oceans and even streets change slowly, so map data can remain relatively current for long periods of time.

But indoors, millions of items on hundreds of thousands of shelves are constantly moving around in tens of thousands of stores. Clerks make changes autonomously to fill empty spaces. Weather conditions may require on-the-fly replacements of barbecue grills from the front of the store with snow shovels, without anyone taking time to update inventory location reports.

Stores are constantly taking new measures to keep location information more current for customers and clerks, but it's a daunting task.

In recent years, there have been several good mobile apps to help with internal mapping in malls and superstores. The key has not been the actual map, because most stores stay relative static in floor plans: The issue is being able to keep current on the location of store items.

Aisle411, one of our book sponsors, is a leader in internal mapping. Nathan Pettyjohn, Aisle411 founder and CEO, told us Aisle411 collects location data on 3.7 million products in 367,000 North American stores including Ace Hardware, The Home Depot, Target, Toys 'R' Us, Walgreens, and Walmart.

Aisle411 uses a Waze-like approach for reporting in-store changes, treating app users as a community of shoppers who inform each other of in-store changes as they experience them, just as Waze users report hazards and slowdowns on highways.

But, until now, Aisle411 has only been able to provide two-dimensional maps for three dimensional stores; it shows locations as they can be seen on a schematic drawing of aisles and shelves, but it can't show you whether the item is on the bottom, top or middle shelf, nor can it display whether escalators in a floor plan go up or down. It can't make it clear what floor you are looking at in a multi-floor department store. The internal maps have been adequate but not optimal.

Aisle411, like Lowe's, is an early Tango partner. It combines Tango's 3D and augmentation capabilities with its own location data to create unprecedented capabilities to find things in stores, malls and eventually other public places.

Although, we don't think the folks at Pokemon Go need to worry much, Aisle 411 has even added a little gamification for shopper entertainment while searching.

We saw an Aisle411 Tango demo at the San Francisco Nordstrom in late beta stages. It showed us how marketing could be integrated into mapping by pretending that singing superstar Taylor Swift had shopped there and bought three items. Shoppers could then use Aisle411 to literally follow Swift's footprints—etched in augmented reality—on the real floor through a Tango device. At each stop, the shopper received reward points just for visiting and bonus points for buying.

The same Tango enhanced Aisle411 app can be used in other ways. Someone arriving at a huge mall could search for cashmere sweaters throughout the entire geofenced mall. Filters can limit the search by style, size or color. Results may show three locations, eliminating 30 others that do not match the criteria.

We believe that phones and tablets are just first steps in Tango's long dance. Eric Johnsen, Tango head of business development, told us that Tango will eventually be in Android-powered headsets and in the infrared eyes of robots such as Lowe's OSHbot.

Tango could also find its way into inanimate objects connected on the IoT. Picture, for example, a Tango-powered shopping cart with a screen showing AR arrows pointing toward desired items and perhaps offering deals on items as you pass by them. This would be easier than pushing a cart with one hand and holding a phone with the other.

This scenario adds marketing possibilities. The cart may not have any of a shopper's personal data, but it does know the item intended for purchase as well as the intended route through the store. Perhaps, by time of day, it knows the shopper may be hungry, or want coffee or an adult beverage. As you pass by the sporting goods section, perhaps Kevin Durant will appear, pointing fans to his new Warriors T-shirts.

The cart will know where shoppers stop en route, hinting at special offers based on context and location. It will select celebrity endorsements more likely to appeal to each shopper throughout the store.

One thing we learned in researching this chapter: Smart brands are already deeply immersed in embracing Fourth Transformation technologies. Our search brought us to many unexpected places, including our first visit to a cosmetics lab.

Virtual Lipstick

Beauty products are a $382 billion global industry, according to *Forbes*, and the category is a highly competitive retail segment. Marketing efforts play to emotions and personalization. The beauty industry turned toward websites and mobile platforms more quickly than most other retail categories.

For example, L'Oréal, Sally Beauty, Sephora and Taaz invite site visitors to upload selfies augmented with virtual lipstick and other cosmetics so that they can see how they look before they buy.

It works the same way cosmetic counters work—except you don't have to leave home and you don't have to smear the stuff on and then wipe it off—and brands don't have to invest in samples. Millions of women have already tried virtual makeup, and AR-assisted sales have picked up accordingly.

Sephora is the innovation leader of cosmetic retailing. The beauty merchant has played the role of disruptor since opening its first shop in 1998.

Before that, makeup was mostly sold in department stores, where brands rented the store counters and provided the sales associates. Because sales reps were often on commission, they were more loyal to products than to customers.

Sephora upended that by eliminating counters altogether, offering products from many brands and letting shoppers try on whatever they pleased in an environment often described as playful. Sales associates are trained to be loyal to customers rather than brands. That changes dynamics. Shoppers are encouraged to stay and sample as long as they wish.

Sephora, like video game makers, realizes that fun is addictive and that it is good for business. Some compare its branded stores to candy stores. A Facebook follower told us that visiting one reminded her of "makeup raids" when her mom was out. "We giggled and made a big mess," she wrote.

The Sephora Lab has built a mock up of a typical retail shop. Twice weekly, sales associates from San Francisco shops visit the warehouse and tell Lab team members how customers might react to proposed tech innovations. When we visited, they were experimenting with digitally developed virtual scents that allowed precise fragrance samplings, without actually applying scented liquids to skin, eliminating the heavy mixture of scents, not always appreciated by passers by.

The current big tech-driven changes are more online and in mobile than in stores. Shoppers are more prone to get beauty tips from over 11 million clips on YouTube than from cosmetic counter clerks. Customers help each other with tips in online communities. Sephora alone has members helping each other via *Beauty Talk*, its online community.

The beauty products industry was driven online a decade ago as social media came in, and the brands joined in on customer conversations. As we mentioned, the most popular single AR application is to see cosmetics applied to uploaded selfies.

Sephora's Bridget Dolan maintains the strategic balance of staying just a little ahead of customers with digital technology.

Sephora has started to use AR in marketing. Shoppers point a mobile app at photos of brand founders, who come to life in 3D, telling stories of how their companies got started.

We asked Dolan when Sephora expected to see AR headsets change in-store experiences. She estimated it would take three to five years and predicted that the first headsets would be provided by Sephora to customers who would probably be experiencing AR for the first time.

We have little doubt that Sephora will be earlier than most beauty brands to take advantage of headsets. We know of at least one startup working on technology to provide virtual scents in headsets, eliminating the need to use valuable store space for sample scents.

But we have been watching AR and VR headset makers become surprised by larger-than-expected headset demand. Dolan may be seeing headset-wearing customer's sooner than she thinks. Sephora may be on schedule to stay a little ahead of competitors, but it may need to hurry up a bit to stay ahead of its customers in this area.

Personal Department Stores

We are always happy to see smaller players coming in with strategies that cause bigger brands to spin around in surprise.

Such is the case with Myers, Australia's largest department store chain, which is partnering with Internet old-timer eBay to create what it calls the *first personal department store*. Myers created an online AR catalog of its most popular products and eBay supplied 20,000 branded Cardboard headsets for Myers' best customers.

The app lets customers see what is in stock in 3D. Then they go online and place orders. The Myers site uses AI to get smarter about each user, remembering their size, what they have visited and bought, and perhaps data about their tastes.

Over time, this can give users a sense that they really are visiting their own personal department stores, stocked only with the products that interest them and as personal as those fabled shops on the Main Streets of yore.

Myers is far from alone in using the new technology to uber-personalize customer experience. Almost all merchants hoping to survive the Fourth Transformation will need to follow suit.

Vanessa Whiteside, head of marketing for London-based Engage Products, published a vision piece in *Huffington Post* where she predicted wearable devices will soon measure all body dimensions. When you shop with smart glasses, you'll see only items that fit you precisely.

Over time—perhaps sometime past 2025—your headset will also have inventory of your closet contents and suggest accessories to go with what you already have.

Resuscitating Consumer Electronics

A decade ago, consumer electronics was among the hottest of hot retail categories, but many factors—particularly online sales—have killed former giants like Circuit City and Radio Shack.

Among the survivors so far has been Best Buy, but it seems to be struggling to redefine itself. It has tried a variety of strategies with mixed success. From our perspective, it announced its most promising play of the last decade in August 2016, when it revealed that for Christmas 2016, it will stake part of its future on virtual reality.

For the 2016 holiday season, the North American chain will be selling Oculus Rift in 500 stores and Sony PlayStation VR in 200. Each store will have demo kiosks where people can try the devices out.

We think it's a good plan. It has been a long time since the chain could claim to be the first at anything, and in this case it will be offering a hot product that is likely to attract Millennials and Minecrafters, two demographics that it will need to attract moving forward.

It also helps Oculus and Sony; the best way to get people to want VR headsets is to get them to try them on for a few minutes. When that happens at consumer and tech shows it is effective, but limited in reach. We think most sales are being generated by early adopters who let their friends try them. Retail kiosks may reach more people whose friends aren't tech champions.

By Christmas 2017, we expect other retailers will follow Best Buy. Selections will probably go beyond VR into mixed reality headsets as well.

Blipp to Buy

There's one more retail dynamic that AR will enable: the concept of the world as your department store, where you can buy clothing off the backs of people you meet socially or even from perfect strangers. You'll stop someone in the street or in a coffee shop and say, "Nice shoes. May I Blipp them?"

It may sound like a pick-up line, but over time it will take on an entirely different context.

You may recall Ambarish Mitra from Chapter 1, where we discussed his vision for a Visual Web 100 times larger than today's worldwide web. Blippar, the company, he started is doing its best to make that vision real.

Founded in 2011, Blippar is a mobile AR app. A user points the phone at an object of interest, and then Blippar analyzes it, attempts to identify it and adds contextual information. Mitra says it behaves like a curious child learning something from whatever it sees.

The Blippar kid is growing faster, and now it can recognize most things it might see in your home or at work or in public places.

Blippar is not just a retail product, but retail represents a huge chunk of its business. When we talked with Mitra, one-third of its 300 employees were dedicated to retail. Blippar is partnering with over 1,000 prominent brands, he told us. When the app sees a logo, it identifies the brand for the user. It can also identify tens of thousands of products; Mitra told us—with some pride—that Blippar can identify every coffeemaker on Earth.

This is the Visual Web. What's the big deal to retailers? It eliminates the sales barrier of languages. A kid in Mumbai sees a LeBron James Cavaliers shirt on a fan visiting the Taj Mahal. Maybe, he doesn't know who James is or what the Cavaliers are. But Blippar lets him click to buy it from a Chinese manufacturer making knock offs.

This is what we mean by ubiquitous shopping. It isn't quite here yet, but it is coming soon.

In November 2016, Blippar and its brand partners launched a "Blipp to Buy" campaign. Shoppers go into stores and buy items off shelves just by scanning barcodes. Payment is automatic. Shoppers just take the items and then leave the store after a scanner confirms the purchase. You can also Blipp to Buy online with equal ease.

The campaign aligns with Whiteside's *Huffington Post* prediction: You will scan body parts to ensure good fits. Soon, ubiquitous shopping will let you buy items in store windows or perhaps from a friend's posted Facebook photo.

Marketers these days are much more interested in what they call omni-channel strategies, in which brands have a presence wherever people happen to be. Blippar is about as omnichannel as you can get.

In the Fourth Transformation, our devices become vital nodes on the IoT. It allows us to communicate who we are, where we are and what we want effortlessly, perhaps automatically.

Not all the consequences of this are positive. But of one thing we are quite certain: The customer experience will be a damn sight better because options will be better. Getting what you want will be easier.

In recent years, consumer markets have driven technologies. For example, consumers were rejoicing in touch-based smartphones while corporate employees were still using BlackBerry phones. People were using social media to help or hurt brands when new products came out, while corporate PR was still issuing press releases that few journalists bothered to read.

So, when our research turned from retail to the business-to-business enterprise, we were surprised to discover that a great many of the world's largest manufacturers and corporations had already been using AR headsets for years.

+++++

CHAPTER 8

Augmented Enterprises

"The only completely consistent people are the dead."

—Aldous Huxley, author and futurist

I f sexy is what you seek, you've come to the wrong chapter. Here we talk about large industrial enterprises, where AR and VR is being used in business-to-business settings and with company employees. It is far different than using MR to help women explore beauty as Sephora does. The enterprise is rarely the sort of venue where Leaping Whales and Pokemon close a sale for you.

In the previous chapter, we talked about big consumer brands dipping their toes into mixed reality technologies before actually taking plunges. Industrial cultures usually take a more conservative approach. They are built upon layers of compliance stacked upon systems and procedures governed by multiple committees that can be quite averse to change.

They are mostly business-to-business entities, and, before they test waters with toe dips, they need to research and compare saline levels, turbulence and the health of overall ecosystems.

This is why new technologies often start with consumers and consumer-facing companies. When the Mac pervaded the home, the office trudged along on DOS- and Windows-based machines for years. When consumers started touching iPhone screens, large enterprise employees were still tapping tiny keys on company-issued BlackBerry phones.

So when we shifted our focus to business-to-business operations, we were surprised not just by how much was going on, but also by how long it had been going on.

It turns out that the concepts for augmented reality began with corporate think tanks as far back as 1968, with large R&D units working on concepts for modernizing global industries even before the necessary technology had been invented.

In 1990, Thomas Caudell, a Boeing researcher, coined the term *augmented reality* to describe the software and head-mounted devices the company had developed to help electricians efficiently and accurately wire the new Boeing 747 jumbo jet.

Since then, augmented reality developers such as ODG, which we discussed in Chapter 4, have been steadily refining AR headsets for the corporation, and steadily growing. How fast and in what direction is hard to sort out. We found estimates for total market size of the AR business by our target year of 2025 varying from IDC's estimate of $162 billion down to Goldman Sachs' more modest estimate of $80 billion, about the current size of the global market for TV sets.

Tom Mainelli, IDC head of devices and displays, wrote in *Recode*, "It is clear, in the long-term view that there are potentially very few businesses that won't be impacted by AR technology."

Such reports did not separate augmented reality from mixed reality, nor did they seem to take into account the probable introductions of significant products from Apple and Magic Leap. We believe when analysts do their projections in 2017, projections will be even higher.

Further, we believe that by the year 2025, both VR and AR will be swallowed into the more elegant mixed reality. And finally, we don't know if current research estimates have taken into consideration the introduction of mobile MR headsets in the next year or two. We believe that when headsets enjoy the same levels of mobility as handsets do today, sales will catapult in nearly all categories.

We do believe, however, that Goldman Sachs is right about 50% of sales being in business-to-business environments, where the value of these devices will be measured in productivity, efficiency and sales, and where their value in relationship to them is beyond dispute.

Researchers are seeing very few mission-critical deployments just yet, but many test projects are still running in low-risk mode. Very often, they start with training manuals. Let's look at a couple such cases:

- **Boeing.** Boeing set up a test in 2016 using two groups that were training to build airplane wings. One used tablets containing an AR version of the manual, while the other used the standard PDF version. The AR group was 30% faster and 90% more accurate.
- **DHL.** PWC reported on a test using AR for order processing in a fulfillment warehouse, where it measured over a similar warehouse using traditional methods. Virtually every person and business has endured experiences where logistics were mission critical. So what DHL learned from its small test has implications to every company that ships goods.

Test results matter. But AR/MR in the corporation faces fewer barriers then in consumer markets. Let's look at couple of those:

- **Price.** While we mentioned consumers balking at prices such as $3,000 for a HoloLens, in the enterprise, the upside potential for savings in productivity, safety, training and quality are so significant that prices are less of a barrier.
- **Fashion.** While consumers are likely to wait for devices that are smaller and less geeky in appearance, this is irrelevant when you view headsets as equipment, like hardhats or welding goggles.
- **Familiarity.** In small numbers, many industrial companies have been seeing head-mounted devices for years. Workers are unlikely to balk at equipment to do their jobs better and in greater safety by wearing headsets.

Hardhats and Helmets

The Daqri Smart Helmet is designed to serve the needs of hardhat workers who must work hands-free. It looks like an ordinary hardhat, except that a smart glass visor is attached to protect welders, plumbers, oil rig workers and others who need to be heads-up and hands-free in factory and field work operations.

The headsets contain sensors that can detect such causes for concerns as pressure buildup in pipes or an error in a complex wiring network. Workers can also attach flashlights or sensor-enabled gas leak detectors when needed.

Like other headsets, the Daqri uses machine learning to know its users on increasingly personal levels, adapting to individual levels of knowledge.

So, a newbie may see every page of a user manual, but when a more experienced worker starts skipping pages, then the headset moves ahead until the eyes show that she's reading. Daqri also catches it if a worker skips an important step and refuses to proceed until it sees the reader complies.

While Daqri's competitive advantage is in the toughness of its smart helmets, there are others that focus on the smartness of tough helmets, the most elegant of which equip pilots of the F-35 Lightning II fighter jet. When a pilot looks, up, down or around, the sophisticated AR device displays a view that converts the plane's fuselage into a transparent form, letting pilots see the ground several thousand feet below or when enemy planes or missiles approach from above or behind.

The new helmets still have a few bugs to work out, including latency in the AR screen that causes airsickness in some of the world's most skilled aviators.

These helmets will be a long time in coming to consumer markets: Current cost is $400,000, and users don't even get a choice of colors. Are they worth the tax dollars? Well, each plane costs over a billion dollars, and millions are invested in training each pilot.

AR helmets are also showing up in other diverse places, with the common thread being protection. STRIVR Labs in Menlo Park, California, makes a helmet to protect pro and amateur football and hockey players from concussion and other impact-related injuries.

Instead of quarterbacks practicing to pass on a field where linebackers practice how to sack them, they play off on their own using AR to emulate a real game. This was originally tested at Stanford University, where a quarterback wearing an AR helmet could simulate the action of a live game recorded with a 360-degree camera rig before 50,000 fans in Stanford Stadium, even though he was actually on the sidelines or in his own backyard.

This helmet is being tested by the San Francisco 49ers and the Dallas Cowboys and by college, high school and elementary school teams.

Concussions and repetitive impact injuries have become an increasing issue for contact athletes. The NFL announced a $100 million program to reduce concussions after the Supreme Court upheld a $1 billion judgment against the League on behalf of 4,500 players who had suffered head injuries.

The AR helmets obviously won't solve all that, but they seem to us to be an intelligent step in the right direction.

Executive Recruiting

Elsewhere in professional sports, we found our first example of VR being used as an executive recruiting tool, and it is one that we believe will find far more widespread use in time.

To recruit basketball superstar Kevin Durant, the Golden State Warriors presented him with a VR headset so he could view what his life as a Warrior would be like. The video, recorded and produced by NextVR, took Durant on a virtual tour of Bay Area attractions including a ride over the Golden Gate Bridge. Durant could watch Coach Steve Kerr chatting with his team and then wander among future teammates on the court and in the locker room.

It seems to us that what the Warriors did to get Durant can be used by almost any organization to woo new talent in an innovative way.

In time, VR/MR will be used by candidates hoping to be hired as well. In a few years, when producing VR videos is as easy as it is today to video record on a smartphone, applicants will start sending recruiters VR videos.

It would be a great way for applicants to...show greater depth.

Augmenting Cars and Drivers

The automotive industry is changing. Much of that change relates to autonomous cars, where each vehicle will be a very large, connected intelligent device.

Every major automaker is moving in this direction, and they are using AR for everything from design concept to repairs and safety checks in the family garage.

Like the aviation industry, carmakers have been using AR and VR in a variety of ways for years.

In 2009, Israel visited Ford Motors and GM for *FastCompany* TV. At the time, he was looking at how carmakers were using social media, but he became fascinated by his introduction to industrial-strength VR and AR in his two factory tours.

At GM, he wore large and clumsy VR glasses that let him see how modifications to the front end of a virtual vehicle could improve or diminish visibility and how paint colors could be tested virtually for sun glare.

At Ford, he saw how AR was used for global collaborative computing. He sat with automotive professionals in a Dearborn, Michigan, auditorium, seeing his first 3D model of a car in the design planning stages on a large flat screen.

Around the world, Ford partners were viewing the same 3D model at the same time. One, a wheel maker in Virginia, wanted a closer look at the rear wheel, which was then magnified on the screen. The brake designer in Ohio asked to view it from multiple 3D angles. They discussed a single rivet that had to be moved for safety reasons. What he saw was not quite AR yet, but it soon would be.

American carmakers are far from alone. Mercedes has been using smart glasses for manufacture and repair since 2008. Audi is doing the same today, as are Lexus and Toyota.

Like DHL and many other companies in factory and warehousing applications, automakers are using AR to streamline logistics. Volkswagen started making 3D glasses standard equipment for all logistical personnel in its main plant as part of a pilot project.

The VW glasses display information such as bin locations and part numbers directly in the user's line of sight, so workers can tell if the part they are looking at matches the part they need. The custom-designed devices have cameras that scan barcodes to further ensure accuracy. This is yet another example of how the new technology improves accuracy, speed and cost.

AR glasses bolster automaker-dealer partnerships as well. Ferrari, Cadillac and Audi have each announced plans for virtual showrooms at dealerships, which typically contain only a minimal number of stripped-down models. Visitors then put on glasses to see colors and options they're considering. This reduces space for dealers and vastly cuts stocking overhead costs.

Manufacturers are also testing online virtual showrooms where shoppers not only look at options, but take virtual drives. When someone is ready to buy, they order at the site, and the car is delivered to an authorized dealer nearby, where the customer can take a real drive before buying.

Even industrial vehicles are embracing AR/VR glasses.

Caterpillar, the world leader in construction vehicles, is extensively using AR/VR in all processes from concept to design, as well as for training, advertising and sales including safety inspections and repair instruction.

The story is similar at John Deere, the leader in farm equipment like combines and tractors. The Illinois-based manufacturer uses both VR and AR for employee and customer training.

Scoble visited the University of Illinois at Urbana-Champagne's R&D Center, where lots of companies, from Mozilla to Tesla, began. Dr. Keith Bujack, who runs Deere's R&D facility at the center, told him, "We are working on all the same things they are working on in Silicon Valley." Much of that is related to IoT. Bujack talked of how each vehicle is a connected device, using sensors to tell farmers about changes in weather, crop nutrition or soil moisture.

We think the proliferation of VR/AR in the automotive industry is indicative of what will happen elsewhere: It will start deep in the industrial side and then wend its way to consumers.

Out-of-World Applications

Just like other makers of passenger vehicles, NASA uses enhanced reality technology at all points along the design and manufacturing cycle. But in space, these technologies get more exciting when placed in the hands of end users.

We already told you about NASA's partnership with HoloLens, and the small steps for educating humankind with a Mars walk demo at a conference. News reports have shown how experts on the ground assist astronauts to make International Space Station repairs via HoloLens headsets.

But NASA says that this is just a beginning. AR glasses will allow Earth-based experts to assist space travelers dealing with whatever they encounter en route or after arriving at extraterrestrial destinations.

One scenario is that non-manned spacecraft will deliver heavy-duty equipment, food supplies and building materials to Mars or some other far-off destination. When astronauts or civilians arrive later, they will use VR manuals to properly use the materials to build and grow what they need.

Space travelers will use AR glasses to communicate with peers, inform the media and educate future space voyagers. All this, less than 50 years after a 16-mm camera used black-and-white film and crackling audio to record the first step for humankind on the moon.

The same type of experience we see taking place in outer space is already helping in the planning and marketing of more pedestrian terrestrial spaces.

Inner Spaces

Skanska USA, a leading development and construction company, partnered with Studio 216, another digital studio, to create this planet's first Holographic Real Estate Center—terrestrially headquartered in downtown Seattle. Skanska is in the midst of a major project in the city, which is emerging as a hotbed for Fourth Transformation development. A third partner, Microsoft, is located nearby.

HoloLens headsets enable potential lessees to take multiuser AR tours of properties before they are built. They can look at a 3D holographic model on a table top, or zero in to examine specific available spaces and even investigate wiring, conduits and pipes.

Skanska is not alone. According to *TechCrunch*, the real estate industry, "never one for embracing new technology," is changing faster with these enhanced technologies than ever before.

Numerous brokers and developers are using the new tech to update the familiar virtual tours that started shortly after the worldwide web emerged. Originally, such tours just used still photos, then photos stitched together, and, eventually, videos. Each step facilitated marketing, making it easy for industry strategists to see the ROI that would result from AR tours.

Now, Skanska and other forward-thinking marketing and leasing operations can start giving tours while a project has not yet evolved past the tabletop model.

Floored, Inc., provides VR software and modeling to commercial real estate developers. In the summer of 2016, Taconic Investment Partners used Floored software on an Oculus Rift headset to market a six-story building in Manhattan before it was completed. The new tenant is Samsung, makers of their own VR headsets.

Once projects are completed, AR/VR will help maintain and preserve them. According to *Construction Week Online,* facility managers are starting to use AR/VR to monitor pipes, wires, and ventilation ducts to prevent such disasters as short circuits or burst pipes. Not only will this reduce maintenance issues, it will also extend building life.

And of course, what starts in commercial spills over into residential. Sotheby's International Realty uses VR to market luxury homes to those with Gatsby tastes and budgets. In the most affluent sections of Manhattan and Los Angeles, affiliates are handing out Samsung Gear VR headsets to serious shoppers. The VR approach is an outgrowth of earlier successful experiments with GoPro 360-degree cameras and 3D scans that allowed virtual walkthroughs.

Doing research on this, we called a broker to ask if we did not buy, would we have to return the headsets? She hung up.

Healthy Outlooks

We've given you a broad overview of a few of the many industries slowly, but decisively, turning toward the new technologies, hoping perhaps to follow the Sephora strategy of staying ahead of customers—but not too far.

We find an interesting reversal of trends. Ever since the first PCs were smuggled into the enterprises of the 1970s, end users have driven new technology, and the enterprise has followed. Now, we are seeing the tech start in the enterprise and flow out to end users.

We have little doubt that whatever type of organization you belong to, your customers and competitors are growing increasingly interested in this new technology. The life of your business may depend upon it soon.

That life may soon be improved and prolonged because of the same technologies. We want to tell you how a little AR game may treat some of the most persistent and devastating of mental disorders.

+++++

CHAPTER 9

To Our Health

"If it's broken, it can be fixed."

—Jeff Abbott, Author of Fear

Researching mixed reality technologies has made us bullish about the future of business. In the two chapters that conclude this book section, we describe huge business categories that will thrive in the Fourth Transformation. The stories we have found are important because of the hope they show for the human condition.

In this chapter we will spotlight healthcare and in the next, education.

Healthcare is certainly big business. In the U.S., according to the *New York Times*, healthcare costs topped $3 trillion in 2014. We are certain the amount has increased, and the Fourth Transformation is unlikely to slow that increase.

What is clear is that virtual reality has already lessened some of the most painful and debilitating aspects of human disabilities and disorders. It also holds out the possibility of cures for others.

Let's start with the healthcare company that impressed above all others.

MindMaze, a Swiss company founded by CEO Tej Tadi, a neurologist with an undergraduate degree in electrical engineering, uses similar virtual reality technologies to simultaneously develop games and ease pain. Evidence is strong that it is succeeding at both.

MindMaze was founded in 2011 as an academic research project; but, by 2016, when it started rolling out products, it had raised over $100 million and was already valued at over $1 billion.

When we talked with Tadi, we had him explain the synergy between games and healthcare.

For gamers, we learned, MindMaze uses patented technology to let players in headsets move things around and zap zombies with brainwaves rather than hand controls. This speeds up the experience in the same way Eye Interaction sped up mole whacking at Eyefluence, except that it is even faster when the motion happens in response to a thought.

On the healthcare side, MindMaze uses similar brainwave headsets to treat amputees, stroke survivors, and victims of irreparable brain and spinal trauma, Parkinson's, cerebral palsy, and post-traumatic stress disorder. Patients using MindMaze show significantly faster recovery speeds than through conventional therapy.

MindMaze uses *motion capture*, a technology used in animated film-making where computer-generated animation precisely mimics an actor's motions. But MindMaze adds a feature called *mirroring*.

An amputee wears a MindMaze MR headset. When she raises her intact left arm, her avatar in the headset raises the right arm, through mirroring, fooling the brain into thinking the amputated limb is still there. This process reduces or eliminates phantom pain, a pain caused by victim brains trying to move limbs that are no longer there.

MindMaze has opened offices worldwide. Its San Francisco office has begun working with amputees at two nearby veterans' hospitals.

Tadi told us that MindMaze will develop unique software for each disorder, all using headsets, neural sensors, motion tracking, machine learning and often mirroring to trick brains and benefit patients.

There are 15 million stroke victims worldwide each year. Stroke is the third leading cause of death in the U.S. Among those who do survive, the speed of recovery is vital. The longer a patient remains in the hospital, the lower the chance of full recovery.

Using the same technology tools that it uses for amputees and burn victims, MindMaze uses mixed reality to trick patient's brains into using limbs again and is succeeding generally faster than traditional physical therapy.

Tadi also maintains that MindMaze teaches patients to move more naturally than the traditional treatment that gets patients home and functioning quickly, physical therapy.

We asked Tadi why MindMaze started in two areas as diverse as amputees and gaming. Reminding us of our earlier observation about the value of fun, he told us that all MindMaze health programs were built on gamification models.

In games, he sees an immediate opportunity. The company's headsets are lighter, more attractive, and less expensive versions of the medical devices, because they don't need to explore the goings-on of the central cortex or read the user's thoughts as the medical version does.

MindMaze will partner with existing game platforms, such as Xbox or Sony PlayStation VR, where gamers will enjoy versions of existing popular titles, but using brainwaves rather than hand controls.

The games and therapy may blur at times, with users not knowing or caring which they are doing. At a San Francisco Gamer conference, MindMaze introduced the headsets as *NeuroGoggles*. A demonstrator used his brainwaves to make flames shoot from his fingers, which may be cool and fun, but, as Tadi told us, will also help schizophrenics control dangerous mood swings.

About 1.1% of the world's population is diagnosed as schizophrenic. In the U.S., treatment costs run about $100 billion annually, and there is no known cure. Tadi told us that MindMaze has a good shot at actually curing the disorder, possibly by 2025.

He told us that MindMaze is also talking to executives in the automotive and defense industries. He believes that the MindMaze headsets could be adapted to enable brainwave override of a bad autonomous car decision. It would have to work really, really quickly.

There are numerous other healthcare approaches using other VR and MR headsets in mixed reality treatments. For example:

- Scientists at the University of Washington have created a game to ease pain in children while their burns are being cleaned out, without the use of pain killers. The kids often say they were not even aware the procedure was happening.

- UCSF Oakland's Benioff Children's Hospital uses a similar approach with VR headsets for children hit by sickle cell anemia, an incurable disease.
- At St. Jude's hospital in Nashville, Expedia, the online travel company, helps children suffering from cancer travel virtually to any destination they choose.

The Brain as Interface

Other organizations are also going to the brain to help the disabled. For example, Braingate is an early-phase company working with Brown, Stanford and Case Western universities. It has reported success teaching quadriplegics to use robotic devices for self-help, making the patients less dependent upon attendants.

Patients use brainwaves to manipulate objects on a tray in front them to feed themselves, brush their teeth, or pour water into a glass and even insert a drinking straw.

There is a long history of using technology to get prosthetic limbs to respond to brain commands as real limbs do. Back in 2001, Israel interviewed Jesse Sullivan, the first bionic man, who actually got to the point where his metallic arm could feel his wife's touch. But his was a long, expensive journey that included frequent hospital visits and prosthetic upgrades.

Since then, there has been slow but steady progress. Patients with the most modern prosthetic hands can use brain power to move artificial fingers more naturally.

In 2014, doctors took another approach. They implanted a chip into the cortex of Ian Burkhart, a college student who had been paralyzed in a diving mishap. By 2016—after two years of trial and error—Burkhart could move by sending brainwaves from the chip to his prosthetic fingers.

There are numerous examples such as these. They may not seem like much, but they each represent significant steps into Fourth Transformation lifestyles in which millions of people will use their brains and intelligent machines to live more independent lives.

We have little doubt that talk of brain implants and brainwave-operated robots and limbs freak some people out today. Even on Facebook, we hear murmurings about the Borg and lamentations of people becoming part heartless machine. We doubt that Jesse Sullivan and Ian Burkhart would agree with the characterization.

The reality is that in 2015, there were 5.6 million quadriplegics and 1.9 million amputees in the U.S. They frequently suffer from pulmonary diseases, bladder control problems, constipation and digestive disorders. They have shorter average life-spans. Hygiene and personal care for these people has not changed much in the previous hundred years.

Only in the last 15 years has the medical science of *neurotechnology*, the approach we have just described, offered much hope.

The 7.5 million people who will be living more normal lives don't care if these mechanical enhancements freak you out or not.

As a matter of fact, they have started to show off what they can do.

The Cyborg Olympics

The Swiss Federal Institute of Technology of Zurich, where MindMaze was incubated, hosted *Cybathlon*, the world's first Cyborg Olympics, in October 2016. It featured teams from 80 countries.

But instead of 1,000-meter relays and pole vaults, participants performed everyday tasks like cutting loaves of bread or opening tightly sealed jars. The purpose was not to compete for gold medals, but to demonstrate the latest developments in technology that help people with disabilities complete daily tasks.

Participants were primarily showing off the latest advances in prosthetic limbs, with most of them brainwave-operated and incorporating AR or VR headsets.

Bionic Exoskeletons

An exoskeleton is an external skeleton that supports and protects an animal's body. You see them on shellfish, insects, turtles and armadillos.

Humans have been devising exoskeletons to perform personal tasks for centuries. Remember those knights in shining armor? Back then, metallic external shells were cumbersome, heavy things; that remained the state of the art for centuries. Lately, Fourth Transformation technologies have made exoskeletons more useful and lightweight.

A company called Ekso Bionics pioneers brain-operated external skeletons for people whose internal skeletons don't properly function.

In a Duke University experiment, eight spinal cord injury victims were able to move limbs and feel sensations for the first time in at least five years by using Ekso Bionic exoskeletons. Users wore a custom VR headset that connects to a backpack computer and, using sensors, to the cortex.

They learned to move the exoskeletons by focusing on VR avatars and making them move, similarly to the way MindMaze does it. Once again, by moving limbs on the avatar, the brain was tricked into believing it could move parts of the exoskeleton. According to Miguel Nicolelis, who headed the project at Duke, once they believed they *could* do it, they actually did it.

The exoskeletons still need refinement. The $40,000 cost remains steep, but it is less than half of what it was when we reported on them in 2012, and the weight has been reduced by more than half to 27 pounds.

Exoskeletal devices are also being used to teach empathy.

The Genworth Aging Experience, sponsored by the insurance carrier Genworth Financial, is an exoskeletal suit on traveling display at contemporary museums. It is called, *"A Walk on the Beach,"* and includes a VR headset that immerses suited-up visitors in an attractive ocean-side setting.

But as they attempt to virtually walk along, the suit adds 40 pounds to their body weight, the average amount of weight an elderly male might put on over the years from their 30th birthday. Their ears ring with tinnitus, an often incurable and annoying distraction in older people. The view of the serene ocean is darkened and obscured by macular degeneration, a vision impairment in millions of older people. The suit applies pressure to joints, simulating arthritis, a disease of many elderly people forcing them to walk stiffly and with pain.

Reuters reporter Barbara Goldberg quoted a museum staff member who observed, "Those who try on the suit often feel they would rather be home in bed than on the beach in the summer's heat."

By the time young visitors reach the geriatric phase of their lives, there may be treatments, or perhaps, even cures for these common debilitations of the elderly. If so, we think there's a good possibility that Fourth Generation technologies will play a role in whatever solutions will be found.

AR/VR in Surgery

In the next chapter, we'll talk about how mixed reality technologies are revolutionizing medical training, as AR and VR better prepare future medical practitioners.

Here we will talk about how practitioners are using enhanced reality technologies to better understand the inner workings of the human body so that they can be more prepared to save lives.

Let's start with AR saving the leg of a cancer victim.

The patient in this case had *pelvic osteosarcoma*, a massive tumor in a hard-to-reach spot. Removing it would have required a difficult surgery that often saves a life, but, just about always, costs the permanent use of a leg.

Timothy Rapp, an orthopedic oncologist, and Pierre Saadeh, a plastic surgeon at the NYU Langone Medical Center, decided to try a route that no one had previously taken. While prior surgeries of this nature entered with incisions from the front of the patient, disabling the leg, they decided to go in from behind. Rapp would then remove the tumor, which was the relatively easy part. The real challenge would be for Saadeh to use plastic surgery to fill the hole left by the cancer with bone shavings, and thus save use of the leg.

When attempting procedures that they have not previously performed, doctors either watch videos of previous surgeries or practice on cadavers. But there had been no previous operations of this nature, and cadavers would not give them the knowledge they needed to save their patient's leg.

Rapp and Saadeh decided that AR would provide the best help.

They contracted software developers to create a high-resolution 3D map of the surgery site, allowing Saadeh to design a method to fill the area through augmented trial-and-error. The method resembles the way architects use 3D mapping to plan out a building's placement on a vacant lot. The map told Saadeh precisely how much space he had to fill. Then he scraped pieces of bone from the patient's leg and used the shavings and plastics to fill the cavity left by the tumor.

They practiced repeatedly before operating. In the actual operation, the procedure worked perfectly. The patient is now home, walking just fine on two healthy legs.

Father of the Patient

Steve Levine is no pioneering surgeon. He is a father of a girl born with a congenital heart disease. His daughter Jesse received her first pacemaker when she was two. By the time she was 25, she was on her fourth.

Levine is also senior director for Dassault Systemes, a global software design corporation. He is based at the firm's labs in Waltham, Massachusetts, where he has supervised 3D simulation projects for customers including Tesla and Boeing.

Motivated by Jesse's condition, Levine built upon two previous projects to create the Simulia Living Heart Project (SLHP).

The center of the project is a precisely replicated VR version of a healthy human heart. Using headsets, med students and doctors can take immersive walking tours of the heart in the same way movie goers can walk around characters in *Remembering Angelica*.

Fast Company's John Brownlee toured the virtual heart in Waltham. He wrote, "From all sides, I am swallowed by this living, beating heart, but I am not in danger. By just thumbing a button at my fingertips, I could easily shrink it down to the size of my hand, or make it disappear entirely."

But, this adventure is intended to save and improve millions of lives. In a few years, doctors will be able to create *digital twins* of organs, so that they can compare a new, healthy kidney to a patient's damaged kidney.

Brownlee asked rhetorically, "Will VR be for medicine what CAD has been for architects?"

As we see it, the answer is a resounding "yes."

Bionic Eyes

There are 285 million blind people in the world, according to the United Nations World Health Organization. This is a significant opportunity for med tech companies and mixed reality developers.

Until recently, the best medical technology could do to help the legally blind was to provide magnifying machines that let them painstakingly read words on printed pages. You couldn't use the magnifiers very easily with computer screens, and you most certainly couldn't take them to the movies or a concert. Perhaps worst of all, you could not see much when you looked into the eyes of loved ones.

But now *bionic eyes* and AR headsets are starting to change the lives of the visually impaired. We found several early-phase *med tech companies* addressing blindness and producing impressive early results.

NuEyes, an Orange County, California, early-phase company, is offering custom software in modified ODG R-7 headsets to restore vision by bypassing damaged retinas.

A camera on the front of the blacked-out glasses serves as the user's eyes. It captures images and magnifies them onto the dark optical lenses, where the wearer views them in HDTV quality.

Obviously, a blind person's eyes cannot properly interact with technologies like Eyefluence. NuEyes uses speech recognition and text-to-speech translations so wearers can hear written words through advanced audio earbuds.

The current price is about $6,000. Perhaps, it will already be lower by the time you read this.

Another promising company in this arena is SecondSight, makers of the Argus II, an AR headset that requires patients to have a tiny sensor implanted behind the retina, creating a bionic eye. The headset sends electrical stimulation to the rear of the retina, which in turn sends visual perceptions to the brain—precisely as an undamaged retina does. The sensor receives visual data from a customized headset, thus letting the brain see what the eye cannot.

AR for the Deaf

AR also promises to provide new hope for the hearing impaired. We attended a HoloLens Hackathon at the *UploadVR* offices in San Francisco where Scoble is entrepreneur in residence.

One hacking group allowed us to see HoloHear, which translates speech into sign language. When deaf people run the app in a HoloLens, they see an avatar using sign language, as well as subtitles.

Amber Murray told us it took the group less than 48 hours to produce the app, which appeared to be ready for use. The version we saw was for English language and signing, but it seems a small task to adapt the software to multiple languages, so that many of the world's 360 million people with serious hearing impediments can benefit.

Kids and Autism

Autism is a term used to describe a spectrum of developmental disabilities in which a person experiences difficulties in understanding social cues.

It hits a special note for Scoble and his wife Maryam because their son, Milan, is autistic. Like other kids with autism-spectrum-related disorders, Milan usually relates and learns better from digital devices than from people.

VR helps such kids in a variety of ways. For example, researchers at the University of Haifa have developed a VR headset app to teach autistic children how to safely cross a busy street; once children practice on VR, they then—with assistance—try crossing real streets.

VR also reads facial expressions, so it can measure an autistic child's attention. In VR, an avatar continues to teach a lesson until the child's attention starts to wander. Then the avatar begins to dissolve, until the child resumes attention and the avatar is restored.

The detachment in autistic children negatively impacts the way they play, which in turn, impairs developmental skills. Zhen Bai, a Ph.D. candidate at Cambridge University, has designed an AR system to encourage autistic children toward more imaginative play.

Children see a mirror image of themselves in an AR screen. They then pick up blocks and sundry objects on a table in front of them, but in the VR viewer those objects become cars, trains or airplanes. The idea is to stimulate imagination in a way that will carry over when the child is not using a headset. The system is in early trials, and results—as of this writing—are inconclusive.

The same sort of approach is used to teach autistic Millennials social skills necessary for success in such situations as job interviews or first meetings with new people, in a project funded by Autism Speaks, a US-based advocacy group. Participants are wired, so changes in brain activity are monitored to see if there is measurable change in cognitive understanding of social behavior.

Dr. Daniel Yang, who designed the program, said sections of the brain associated with social understanding come to life during sessions after having lain dormant for years.

Ten Years Hence

Everything we have told you about in this chapter is still in its early phase. In terms of medical processes, they have as yet proved very little.

But they provide great hope, a hope that has been long denied to patients with some of the cruelest medical conditions in the world and to those who love and care for them.

While enhanced reality technologies may actually cure nothing, the treatments indicate that those who are disabled may become more autonomous, those who suffer agonizing pain will suffer less and those whose survival depends on surgery may live better in the future than was possible in the recent past.

This same technology is helping not just the patients, but a whole new generation of medical practitioners, who may be more experienced and confident before they ever touch you or someone you love.

We get even more optimistic when we see how these technologies are already being used to train the medical practitioners of tomorrow and potentially everyone else.

+++++

CHAPTER 10

Teacher, Virtual Teacher

"We must teach our children to dream with their eyes open."

—Harry Edwards, sports sociologist

The way we teach has remained mostly the same since the time of Socrates. The instructor talks, the students listen and then the person in front of the room asks questions. This has been a successful method for many years, starting in preschools and continuing through on-the-job training for skilled professionals.

But who among us has not sat in such a classroom and felt our minds wandering, drowsiness mounting, and a yearning to be somewhere else far away? How many lessons have you had that you forgot as quickly as your notebook or computer closed?

Mixed reality offers the greatest hope in many centuries of improving how people learn. We talked about it earlier in Chapter 8 when we described how Caterpillar, John Deere and Boeing use headsets to help workers learn and retain better.

Now similar techniques are coming into the world's classrooms, promising to keep students immersed in ways more memorable than the way Socrates taught. This is no knock to the venerable Greek teacher, but a tribute to the capabilities of Fourth Transformation technology

And it is easy to see how that would work. Instead of memorizing dates and places, students can be virtually present as William the Conqueror takes down his kid brother at Hastings or look over King John's shoulder as he signs the Magna Carta. They can sail the ocean blue with Columbus. A classical music student could even play a Paganini opus with the London Philharmonic.

Replacing Cadavers

VR as a teaching tool is likely to transform all levels of education from grade school all the way up to advanced medical schools, where it has begun changing how future surgeons will learn their craft.

A med student will use virtual reality to become adept and experienced with cardiovascular anatomy, long before making incisions into the chest of someone you love.

Case Western Reserve University and Cleveland Clinic are partnering to develop a new 485,000 square foot health education campus intended to be the world's most advanced medical teaching facility. A university spokesperson said it prides itself on developing programs that other med schools emulate.

For now, its technology flagship is HoloLens, which will replace cadavers with mixed reality. Instead of cutting open corpses, medical students will use the headsets to virtually cut into realistic live organs and tissue. HoloLens launched the project in April 2016 at the Microsoft Build developer conference in San Francisco.

It began with Professor Pamela B. Davis, Case's dean of medicine, who showed a hologram of a six-foot tall male standing on the dais. Two students joined her as she demonstrated the new way they will learn.

Davis used a simple gesture to zoom into the abdomen, where she spotlighted the stomach, liver and intestines. Then, with a second gesture, she spun the holographic figure around 180 degrees, letting students immediately identify the pancreas and learn where to find it.

A third gesture allowed Davis to enlarge the pancreas by removing it from the figure in the form of a separate hologram that rotated slowly in mid-air, showing med students how to identify it from all angles.

The demo then showed most of what is inside the human body, from brains to bones, so that students could not just locate, identify and examine, but also practice repairing and replacing broken or damaged parts.

HoloLens and other headsets can use this same approach in diverse cases where hands-free instruction has obvious benefits: cooking, welding or repairing expensive machinery. 3D sensors can alert you to correct mistakes. It is how Saab is training future sea captains to steer ships before they go to sea.

Case Western also plans to use HoloLens for distance instruction for remotely located medical students at other med schools. The school demonstrated how this will work at the Microsoft Build conference, where instructors appearing to be on stage in San Francisco were actually holograms presenting from Ohio.

We see the world's most qualified instructors in such varied topics as art history, civil engineering, ceramics, environmental science, gardening or home repair teaching in the classrooms of the world and interacting with students in those classrooms, while actually delivering lectures from the comfort of their own homes.

We like the idea of live AR instruction even more than VR video in two very common cases:

- **Engagement.** Topics such as anatomy require interaction to be effective. Having a human instructor interacting with students is clearly a benefit.
- **Frequent Change.** VR video is expensive to produce, and will probably remain that way for at least five years. If you are teaching current events, economics or political science classes where the content is likely to change rapidly, then it makes more sense to have human holograms rather than VR videos.

But VR is still effective for many types of classes, including for public school students.

Virtual Learning Tours

In the west, there are two big players working on VR learning. They are taking similar approaches and are destined for the sorts of competitive clashes that accelerate innovation while lowering costs.

Google Expeditions is a kit for teachers who want to take their pupils on virtual field trips. It uses Cardboard viewers and Alchemy VR software to provide 3D tours of more than 200 destinations including coral reefs, Antarctica, space, museums and landmarks like Buckingham Palace.

The 360-degree panoramas and 3D images are annotated with details, points of interest and questions for students.

In the Buckingham Palace production, Expeditions takes children on a virtual tour similar to what actual visitors see on real palace tours, soaking in grand ballrooms, great works of art and polished storytelling by virtual docents.

Today, the kits are expensive: A 30-student module that includes a VR ViewMaster that shows 3D still photos, Cardboard, and other teaching tools retails at Best Buy for $10,000.

We imagine sales are starting in more affluent school districts.

Nearpod is the other current player. It is a fast-growing learning company backed by a group of investors that include Salesforce CEO Mark Benioff. The company is taking a similar approach to Expeditions, with virtual reality software viewed on Cardboard by grade school children in thousands of US schools. It also takes kids on educational tours of global current and past wonders including Easter Island, the Great Pyramids, the Great Barrier Reef and the world's tallest buildings.

Nearpod appears to be less expensive than Expeditions with license packages starting at $1,000, and the company provides some economically deprived districts with kits for free.

We can't judge the merits of these two programs, but we have to admit we favor Nearpod. In Lethal Generosity, Israel wrote about urban U.S. school districts where students could afford neither school supplies nor hot lunches. Donating modern supplies to these students seems to us one way to bridge the much-lamented digital divide.

Immersive VR education is not yet as significant a player as Nearpod or Expeditions, but we like the way it uses VR storytelling. One of its first productions, a VR version of the Apollo 11 flight to the moon, won a Unity Vision Award for the Best Film of 2016. Because Unity provides the platform used by nearly every VR game developer, its award gives Immersive additional credibility.

Fun with Chemical Compounds

zSpace, another educational startup, builds VR labs for public schools. Their system involves a touch-sensitive monitor with an inkless cursor pen that students use to tap and draw on the screen. They wear 3D glasses that let them experience a variety of topics more immersively than is possible on a flat screen.

Sixth graders in the Utica County, Michigan, school district draw animations that move with a natural fluidity. In preparation for tomorrow's med school, kids can take tours of a human heart or the inside of an eyeball or disassemble and reassemble a bionic arm. When they tap on an object, a text box pops up to explain details.

The labs are designed for schools and can be used for new forms of quizzes. In one, living creatures appear, such as a preying mantis or a manatee, and the kids need to identify them as insects and marine mammals respectively.

Of course much educational AR and VR will begin to appear on the phones and tablets that are already everywhere. We would be surprised if Google's Tango-sensor-equipped mobile phones did not introduce a suite of 3D programs for child and adult education.

And where there are phones, there must be apps. Books & Magic plans to sell children's illustrated classic books in paper versions and has started with *The Little Mermaid* told in the time-honored words of Hans Christian Anderson. But the book is filled with new artwork, and when the child hovers the phone with the mobile app over the picture, the photo springs up in a 3D rendering. The mermaid almost reaches out and touches the reader.

We found a really cool app that teaches one of the toughest lessons we recall from high school, one of the many we promptly forgot shortly after passing the test: Arloon Chemistry uses AR to teach what elements make up common compounds, such as hydrogen and oxygen to make water. The clip is fun and entertaining, two qualities that we found lacking in the classroom when we studied chemistry.

Virtual Teachers

China has done more than most countries to slow its population growth, in no small part through social engineering. Since 2005, its annual population growth rate has stayed below half of one percent per year. But with its population of nearly 1.4 billion, there are still seven million babies born each year. Most will go to public schools.

This creates a problem: While China is aggressively recruiting and training teachers, it has been unable to keep up with the growing pupil population.

The gap concerns a government and a parental culture that make quality education a top priority. What viable alternatives exist for teachers in the classroom? Perhaps virtual teachers.

NetDragon, a successful hack-and-slash video game developer, sees a potentially bigger market in educating kids than arming them to slay video monsters and pirates. In cooperation with the government, it has been developing virtual teaching software for use with headset-equipped kids in classrooms where there are no teachers.

The developer has been developing and experimenting with the idea since 2013, and in 2017, China will try out entire AR classrooms in a few places to see how they work.

There is, of course, more to being a teacher than just teaching. Teachers need to be keen observers of which students need special attention, or tougher discipline. The NetDragon teaching headsets will use sensors to watch each student's behavior on a one-to-one basis. Teaching will be slowed down for students who need to go at a slower pace and sped up for smart kids who might get easily bored.

To keep kids on their toes, the program can spring a pop quiz on any kid at any time.

Virtual teachers will have a certain objectivity, playing no favorites and adjusting to styles that seem to work best for the students. Each pupil gets to select the gender and age of their instructors and can change whenever they choose. Perhaps, over time, AI will allow the personalities to evolve, allowing the software to play sterner or more entertaining roles as the situation may call for.

Headsets, as we have reported, can often detect some learning disabilities such as autism at earlier phases than a human teacher might.

This raises the issue of privacy. In China, most people are accustomed to a government that watches its people closely in the name of preventing social unrest.

But AI-powered headsets spying on children may be met with strong objections in the West. In coming years, we may just find out.

In August 2016, NetDragon acquired British online education provider Promethean World for $100 million. Promethean serves 2.2 million teachers and 40 million pupils worldwide with AR applications for handheld devices and smart whiteboards. It is big in countries such as India, which place a high priority on child education as population increases make it hard to train enough teachers quickly enough.

Prometheus' main business is in providing smart whiteboards for classroom use. These smart boards are capable of showing VR or AR to entire classrooms, but do not have sensors and do not see the eyes of each student.

It remains to be seen how these smart boards will fit into NetDragon's plans, but the company is in a good position to improve the future of child learning in a large percentage of the world.

Secret Sauce

How and what we teach our children determines not just who they will grow up to be, but also how they will affect our communities and how our culture will develop and change.

Writing about the future of learning on the *Singularity Hub* blog, Jason Gantz observed, "VR education will allow us to learn faster and more interactively than ever before. And VR collaboration spaces will allow us to work from anywhere to solve the world's grand challenges."

We think Gantz gets to the soul of these new technologies, the secret sauce that makes mixed reality technologies so much better than what has preceded them.

We learn and communicate faster, more enjoyably and with deeper understanding than has ever been possible. If we were to boil down the essential point of this book, it's that everything can be learned and communicated better via Fourth Transformation technologies. AI is the engine of this new era, and in most cases, it works best in a headset, rather than a handset.

Even though we write as unabashed tech champions, our vision of these new technologies is not entirely rose colored. There are aspects of having human teachers replaced by brain-reading software that chills us as parents and grandparents.

In fact, there are other causes for concern as well. There will be those who abuse the new technologies for personal gain and, as has always been the case, there are potentially dark and troubling side effects.

Let's take a look.

+++++

PART 3

World Changers

"The people who are crazy enough to think they
can change the world are the ones who do."

—Steve Jobs, entrepreneur/inventor

CHAPTER 11

What Could Possibly Go Wrong?

"The saddest aspect of life right now is that science gathers knowledge faster than society gathers wisdom."

—Isaac Asimov, science fiction master

We are talking about technology that connects directly to our brains, watches what we watch, maintains data on our personal patterns. It knows when we are aroused or bored. It can detect when our heart beats faster or stops entirely.

What could possibly go wrong?

Most future-focused books have dark-side chapters. This is ours.

This is our third book together. In our previous two, we looked at the possible downsides to social media and contextual technologies and shrugged them off. Perhaps, our tone was a bit smug. Our defense is that we write, not as objective observers, but as tech optimists.

The way we see it, disruptive technology always has damaging side effects but has always made life and work better. Always. We remain certain of this after having spent two years looking at the amazing new technologies delivering us into a new era.

But, to tell you the truth, some of the dark-side possibilities of artificial intelligence and mixed reality scare the crap out of *us*. There are deep and disturbing things that can go wrong in this new age where people and machines become so closely intertwined.

Our first fear, is a bit egocentric:

What if we are wrong?

We were right when we argued that social media would change how companies and customers communicated in *Naked Conversations*; we were right again when we said mobile, social, the IoT, data and location technologies were converging to help businesses understand customer needs better, but privacy was at risk, in *Age of Context*.

Are we right this time when we say people will abandon handsets for headsets and that the user interfaces will be the world around each of us?

Maybe the VR and AR that people will enjoy with Tango, Snapchat and Pokemon Go will prove to be so engaging, that it will satisfy them enough to not want headsets.

It could be that the headsets do not improve in design and capability at the accelerated rate we predict. It could be that they do not achieve the mobility that is so important to the Fourth Transformation. It could be that Magic Leap and Apple deliver disappointing devices or nothing at all.

It is possible that no technologist will figure out how to produce that single pair of smart glasses that contains all the necessary technology in a small enough device to make smart glasses that will not be discernible from ordinary glasses.

Also, it could be that the other Fourth Transformation technologies such as self-driving cars, robots and other AI-powered devices are just too freaky for most people, and the whole thing fizzles.

But if all that happened—if any of it happened—it would go against almost everything we found during our two years of research. It would go against a history of digital technology going all the way back to the first personal computers. It would mean that the best and brightest technologists of today are unable to build upon the foundations of the best and brightest technologists of yesterday. There's just too much to gain, and too many smart investors, companies and technologists betting on it, for this future to fizzle.

While it is probable that some of our specific predictions will not unfold as we have written about them, the evidence is overwhelmingly compelling that we are entering into a very different world, one driven by AI and mixed reality technologies, and there is simply no turning back.

That being said, we have concerns that this relentless progress will lead to issues related to health, safety, privacy, marketing clutter, and the possible Orwellian isolation of individuals.

Such factors could result in people wanting to either just turn the damned things off and let progress leave them behind, or worse, become hopelessly addicted to mixed reality experiences.

Let's fast forward ten years. The world of MR has arrived with a variety of headsets that show you wondrous virtual things mixed into the real world.

Fashionistas are loving the contemporary headset designs by Polo, Von Furstenberg and Gucci. People can choose from large selections at LensCrafters, Warby Parker, Target, Costco and Walmart. Tango interior maps point them to what they want or robot clerks guide them to their desired items. Choices are abundant and competition is fierce, so special offers abound.

This is our vision of the near tomorrow. What could possibly go wrong? Well, for one thing, the experience of childhood could change into something that we grownups can't even recognize.

Avatars for Role Models

In our previous chapter we characterized headsets as *super teachers* for the world's children, capable of appearing as avatars customized to suit your children's tastes. These devices will know when your kid is inspired or bored; they will never lose patience or have to slow the pace if your child is a quick learner.

But can teaching systems be corrupted to conform to hidden commercial or government agendas? Of course they can. What about the culture that results when children trust software more than humans? How will we feel when our kids have avatars for role models? How does society change when children with these perspectives grow up and guide global culture?

Then there's the influence of religion and politics. There's always politics. In the U.S. there are school boards that would prefer teaching intelligent design over science. Could they opt to allocate funds for paper bibles rather than holograms that show that climate change is not God's will?

We talked about China, where the demands of a growing population may make it the first country to use educational headsets to replace teachers.

How will those children grow up? When they want to learn something, will they turn to virtual instructors on headsets? How does this change learning?

Will such a system teach them to be creative, or will they emulate the behavior of robots? It's not just children; while human chefs often inspire students to generate creative recipe changes, we fear that automated instructors may teach precision and thus remove many joys of cooking.

This is not an issue that affects only children. All sorts of adult learning will be conducted in mixed reality. Training manuals will be in VR, the safety of wiring commercial airplanes and buildings will depend upon AR and VR. Traditional companies like Caterpillar, DSL and John Deere will be using it to train new workers. Will there be no future need for the "old Joe" of the workplace, the voluntary mentor who helps the new hires understand the nuances of company culture and job performance?

We won't know the consequences of such practices until they become more widespread, as they most certainly will be in the next decade or so.

Come to think of it, tech has been changing how and what we learn since shortly after the birth of the microprocessor.

Today, our devices store the phone numbers for the people we call or send text messages to. In the past, we memorized them.

There will soon be robo-cars. Eventually, people may not have to know how to drive. There will be no need to know the directions to where you want to go. There will be no need to use Waze to find the best routes. Our cars will handle all that through connections to other cars, infrastructure brought to you by IoT, and systems like Uber or Lyft.

What will we do with all that brain space that is about to be freed up? Will our brains become more creative or intuitive, or will the cubbyholes of our cerebellums start to deteriorate and grow dank and dusty like some dark corner in the cellar?

Will we become smarter or dumber in the Fourth Transformation?

An Entertaining Future

Limited time and space in this book have required us to narrow our focus to mixed reality technology. Artificial intelligence in the Fourth Transformation also includes autonomous cars and robots, intelligent software and devices that talk with us and things not yet invented such as shopping carts that use MR interior 3D maps on screens fixed to the carts. They guide you to your destinations in stores, while making pinpoint marketing suggestions.

There are also the vital, connected inanimate IoT sensors, each of which individually contains just a speck of intelligence. But collectively, they are far smarter than even Watson, the world's most intelligent machine.

Each of these changes eats human jobs. John Markoff, in *Machines of Loving Grace*, noted that until 2015, tech had created more jobs than it had eliminated. Moving forward, he doubts that will remain true; we share his concern, despite the potential for creating millions of jobs in mixed reality in media creation, entertainment and marketing.

There has been concern about the loss of jobs to machines for many years. Science fiction writer Arthur C. Clarke envisioned a world in *Childhood's End* where government efficiently distributed wealth so that all people had whatever they needed.

If Clarke was right, then we worry about where VR entertainment has headed thus far and how it will impact ethics and culture moving forward.

In his world, the new leading industry was entertainment, in which creative people were employed to keep unemployed masses amused in their abundant leisure time. Will this kind of entertainment fill the empty spaces of the brain where phone numbers once dwelled? Would it be better to just let them go dark?

Right now, the fastest growing entertainment segment in VR is games, where a very large portion of the activity includes slashing, stabbing, zapping and shooting. Could all this gamified butchery inspire some real-world horrors? Will this make players insensitive to real violence, as some argue TV has done?

Killing Ugliness

There are other troubling aspects of MR technologies. It replaces what is really there with something that is not, and it is getting so good that you will not be able to tell which is which.

This capability created many of the most exciting experiences we've described in this book, but leaves us with a residue of concern.

When we see something ugly, can we simply replace it with a vision of a butterfly or waterfall? If we find ourselves in unpleasant surroundings, can we simply say the words "put me in Yosemite," and immerse ourselves into more pleasant surroundings?

We are concerned that MR will kill ugliness in the same way smartphones have killed boredom.

What will this mean to humans who can avoid unpleasantness with a gesture, word or simply by moving their eyes? Will we lose empathy, even as AI devices gain it? If that is true, will children of tomorrow turn to devices rather than parents for comfort?

Will government make ugly neighborhoods look attractive with virtual flowers, windows or settings masking the suffering of humans who live there? Will a homeless person sleeping in a doorway still be there, while people walking by see a beautiful potted plant? How will that impact compassion or outrage?

The possibilities chill us.

Virtual Sex

When we look back on the two years since Scoble started talking with technologists about coming changes, we have had many conversations that would later haunt us. A couple hover before us like ghosts in a VR experience at The Void.

One such conversation was with Meron Gribetz, CEO of Meta. He talked about how good his company's mixed reality headsets were at replacing reality with illusion and the use of haptic technology to allow users to actually feel people who were not really there.

Israel asked him a theoretical series of questions: "If there was a lonely teenage boy who never had a girlfriend and wanted one, could he have a virtual girlfriend? Could he personalize her to his anatomical, intellectual, spiritual and aesthetic tastes? Could she be programmed to do nothing but please him, including sexually?

The answer to each question was: "Yes."

Hmm. Could he end up preferring the virtual girlfriend to a real one?

"Yes," came the answer. But Gribetz, like us, had no idea what the social implications of that would be, and it was only later that we realized that if virtual sex became preferred to the real kind, there was a threat to the preservation of the human race.

This is already happening in Japan, where young people are less interested in taking mates and having children, and the birth rate is below the replacement rate. The country is becoming more elderly and less productive, and its economy is faltering.

Another friend, Martin Varsavsky, is starting a company in Madrid that will enable people to reproduce without having sex at all, giving a whole new meaning to "the right to choose."

Such talk about not making babies the old-fashioned way reminds us a bit of Aldous Huxley's dystopian 1932 classic, *Brave New World*, where babies are manufactured in laboratories. New babies are designed for lives performing whatever task the government thinks society needs. Many will be worker drones, while a select few will lead, enforce or manage factories.

Huxley also created a precursor of VR sex replacing the human kind in the form of a virtual entertainment called *feelies*, where people went to movie theaters and got their sensations and satisfaction by feeling the experience of sex being performed in the film.

Government Control

Huxley's main theme, however, was of government control, and that concerns us even more than the disappearance of sex as we now know it. He paints a world of governmental uber-control over everyone and everything.

If you are depressed in his brave new world, the government supplies you with an edible substance called Soma that cures your depression, because it is easier to control happier people. We were reminded of that when we researched MindMaze and other medical technology companies who are using mixed reality to ease pain and treat terrible diseases and disorders.

But how could a government use it to control society?

In the previous chapter, we talked about China and government-sanctioned virtual teachers, a program which has clear benefits when human teacher supplies are limited. Will these trusted pieces of AI software teach children to see the world as their government wants it to be seen? It is entirely possible.

Could the U.S. Department of Health and the insurance industry lobby partner with the Pokemon folk to create a subversive exercise program based on trophy hunting. Could the trophies become small tax deductions for the most adept players or when certain weight reduction milestones are reached?

This sounds cool and fun. Improving education and getting people to exercise are noble causes, even if a little subliminal government manipulation is involved. But, as we have noted, once something *can* be done, it probably *will* be done. Could government, intent on its own preservation, or aggressive marketing organizations intent on corporate profits, use AR and VR to manipulate citizen behavior? In fact it has already been done by Facebook, and we would guess others.

It is certainly possible unless safeguards are built into the new technology, and we hope that will happen, but so far it has not.

Are virtual girlfriends the feelies of the near-term future? Could governments start using VR games and rewards to control society for better or worse? We think that something along these lines will happen before the year 2025.

We wonder what Huxley would say, if he were around to watch this Fourth Transformation.

Facebook Worriers

Since we published *Naked Conversations* in 2006, we have used social media to get insights, feedback and ideas from our online friends. We post early draft excerpts of our books to get suggestions before we go through editing and polishing.

This transparent process has sometimes embarrassed us, but it always helps us write better books.

We asked questions on Facebook as we wrote through late 2015 until nearly the end of 2016. The most active response came when we asked Facebook friends what scared them about the new technologies. We received over 100 suggestions.

Roger McNamee, an investor and rock guitarist, told us, "I worry that prolonged exposure to VR will lead to undesirable neurological side effects. I worry that policy makers are too ignorant and lazy to prepare for massive social change. I worry that the leaders of Silicon Valley lack empathy."

So do we.

Deirdre Porter, CEO of MiMic, a mobile app, was concerned about human disconnection: "We already live in a disconnected multi-device world. What if we take a connection between 'virtual violence' and real violence with a grain of salt? There are crazy gamers who may confuse play war and real war. Will kids playing virtual war games develop a form of Post Traumatic Stress Disorder?"

Porter makes a good point, and it could be worse than that: Will people do abhorrent things because their mixed reality screens made it seem like fun?

Later in this chapter, we'll give you an example of how this might roll out when we tell you about how the Pentagon may conduct future real wars that won't seem much different from the ones enjoyed in VR games.

In a world where what is real blurs with what is not, there will be many possible twists. Could hackers have fun by putting a gang of virtual terrorists in an airport? Absolutely. So, after experiencing a practical joke by hackers, do people grow accustomed to seeing the images and not know when the real thing takes place?

People have long demonstrated what craziness can result when illusion replaces reality. Back in the golden days of radio, the actor Orson Welles read an adaptation from H. G. Wells' science fiction book *The War of the Worlds*. People in New Jersey fled their homes, panicked that Martians were attacking.

Robbers, Scammers and Spammers

Fictitious characters may be great for movies, books and other story-telling media. But when you encounter characters in real life who are not who they seem to be, the experience can quickly move to the dark side.

There were certainly malicious imposters long before the advent of the Fourth Transformation. They greeted you with smiles and called you "friend" before revealing themselves to be scammers, swindlers, flimflam artists, hackers, phishers and terrorist recruiters.

They have lurked wherever decent folks have gathered. Often they look just like everyone else, but they are not who they seem to be.

Until now, they have always been human at least, and they could be detected by flaws in the roles they played. But what happens when the phishers and swindlers use appealing, righteous avatars to bilk people like you and us?

We can only imagine.

Of this we are certain: Hackers and pretenders will flock in great numbers to the new technologies, because that is where bad guys can most easily extract money from the innocent. It is so much safer and more profitable to scam in VR than to pull a ski mask down over your face and point an automatic weapon at a bank teller, and if you get caught, the penalties are likely to be smaller.

We are not convinced that law enforcement officials will become experts at patrolling illegal activities online in the next decade; they are already having such a tough time of it in the real world. On the other hand, it will be harder for law enforcement to profile people by race, gender or sexual preference when everyone can appear as anyone.

Of course, there are more than a few dangers if the woman you think you are interviewing as a potential roommate turns out to be an armed predator.

Inevitably, there is a more pervasive threat from people who are not criminals, but are known to be devious. They, too, gather wherever decent folks can be found. They, too, smile and act like your friends.

We are sure you have encountered them and were not always pleased with the experience. They are called marketers.

Virtual Barkers

First, a qualifier: Some of our best friends really are marketers. We know, trust and respect a great many members of the profession, and we both have been known to take advantages of special offers that have popped up while we were online.

Israel spent 20 years as a PR and marketing executive. He has been writing and speaking about technology enabling marketers to be more conversational and less intrusive since the late 1990s.

That being said, there remain far too many marketers, advertisers and PR practitioners whose strategy is a game of numbers. They believe that the most noise produces the most sales, and that is how they get measured and compensated.

They can show you that with response rates of less than 1% on massive, spammy campaigns, they can measurably boost company sales and brand awareness. The catch is that they overlook the collateral brand damage done by pissing off 99% of the people they reach in such campaigns.

While, some marketers are wisely using filters to focus on people likely to want marketing messages, we are worried that others will use location technologies, IoT headsets and software to bombard anyone within range.

This may not be the most dangerous of the problems that we discuss in this chapter, but it is one that we believe will be commonplace in the Fourth Transformation.

In Chapter 4, we talked about Pinpoint Marketing, an effective way to talk with customers on a scalable one-to-one basis, based on an understanding of location and personal data.

Some of that is happening already, and we expect more will occur as we drive forward in the coming decade. But there are many more persistent online peddlers, the ones we call *plaid-suit merchants*, who will target consumers with combinations of ads, offers, notifications, instructions, alerts and videos that play automatically and are difficult to turn off.

We hope that in this coming new era, you will have the tools to filter them out of your otherwise great experiences. But to date, we are aware of no such filters or tools, and there is a danger that this ugliness will persist.

Keitchi Matsuda, founder of the Critical Design studio, has produced a series of film clips that depict the potential for a glaringly ugly world of mixed reality where every conceivable space is doused in a confetti of sales messages: Every product you pass by on shelves, windows and on the streets hit you with notifications and offers.

Irena Cronin is the editorial director for the VR Society, a division of the Advanced Imaging Society, which formed in 2009 as a collective effort of companies including Disney, Warner Brothers, DreamWorks and Sony to advance stereoscopic 3D content. She is another Facebook friend who shared her concerns over what could possibly go wrong.

Cronin talked about "customer dumbification," in which every marketer assumes every person within range of any given location should get suggestions and instructions. The Matsuda clips depict what she means in vivid ugliness.

In one, the mixed reality headset wearer is at home making tea, as a pop-up notice delivers step-by-step instructions on how to heat water, pour it into a cup and then drop in the teabag—and so on. She is cautioned by a somber voice that splashing hot water on her hand could cause scalding.

Matsuda's clips depict a disturbing future in which life in smart glasses would be like being perpetually in Times Square at midnight on New Year's Eve—except there is no cause for celebration.

The potential is worse than just the interruption. As Rob Thompson, one of our Facebook followers, wondered, "What happens when the marketers know when the ad makes your hearts tick quicker?"

We can think of few answers that will serve to lessen any concerns you might have. Historically, there has been a Cold War between the plaid-suit merchants and online users. The merchants find a way to get to you, and technology finds a way to block them. VR is just another front in that battle.

Danger in the Tech

Marketers aside, we see danger in the technology itself in areas where machine intelligence—and the people who program it—are over-rated.

McNamee told us, "I worry that AI will be programmed by people whose limited life experience and awareness blind them to how the real world works." For example, people don't really come to full stops for commuter traffic lights when getting onto freeways. A self-driving car probably would, perhaps getting itself rear-ended because the human driving the car behind it doesn't comply with the letter of every traffic regulation; most people just use common sense.

He has a point: Right now AI seems to be able to demonstrate greater empathy than common sense. In September 2016, someone posted a photo of a naked child on Facebook. Faster than any human could have done it, the social network's policing software bots took down the offending content— just as it was trained to do.

Except that in this case, the photo had won the Pulitzer Prize. Taken in 1972, it is among the most memorable images of the Vietnam War. It shows children fleeing their village after it was hit by napalm bombs. One child is a naked girl; her face is etched with terror.

Two days later, humans at Facebook wisely reversed the decision and apologized, which it seems to us, displays common human sense.

Cronin, observed, "Until machine learning delivers fine-grained results, the potential for an oversimplified understanding of things through coarse-grained categorization is very high. Also, current machine learning error rates could lead to confusion."

Hacking on the IoT

It scares us that hacking software, or *malware*, can essentially tamper with anything that is connected to the Internet of Things.

This has led to a few pranks, such as teenagers making lights in a neighbor's home flicker, or the fun of causing the toilet water to spray someone seated on a $4,000 My Satis, a smart toilet, as it makes screeching noises.

In 2015, IoT malware creators came up with something new called ransomware. First it was used to seize personal computer data and hold it for ransom, usually for about $200.

In 2016, ransomware got more devious: It started holding confidential medical records hostage until insurance companies paid a ransom to the tune of $20 million.

But there is greater fear that medical industry vulnerabilities could make it easy for malicious hackers to seize control of connected instruments and hold them hostage until payment is electronically sent to an untraceable source. An insulin pump could be disabled until a payment is made—a surgical robot could be stopped midway through a procedure in the same way.

But it goes further still. The IoT is, of course, the backbone of the Fourth Transformation, and Internet of Things devices are often less than completely secure. But these hacking attempts have been traditionally stopped with software patches, something every PC and mobile device user knows about and lives with.

How do you update an IoT radio out in a field with no smartphone towers nearby? It's impossible.

As medical devices, toilets or inevitably smart glasses become targets, it may be more difficult, take a longer period of time and cost more to stave off the bad guys.

This brings us to the very real threat of cyber terrorism. Evidence is compelling that the Russian government has tried to tamper with the 2016 election through cyber hacking.

Could cyber terrorists hack air traffic control towers at peak traffic times when multiple jets are landing or taking off? Could they jam all life-saving connected devices in a large hospital or black out entire northern cities on a freezing night?

How far will this go in a society that may soon rely on mixed reality imagery to even buy milk? While no one knows, we certainly see headsets as devices that could become vulnerable because they provide access not just to personal data, but also to people's brains.

Brain Hacks and Predictions

Brain hacking uses simple tricks to improve memory, reasoning, mental fluidity, productivity, energy and mood, as we described with MindMaze. Some approaches now in planning stages involve controlled electric jolts to the cranium and chip implants that will enhance or bypass damaged— or aging—brain sectors. Both approaches are intended to enhance mental capabilities.

Many of the VR, AR and mixed reality applications we've talked about involve brain hacks that make your brain think that it sees something or someone who is not there.

All of these seem to us to be good ideas. The question we have now is, how else could brain hacking work? Could one person's memory replace someone else's so that an innocent person remembers committing a crime and thus confesses? Could virtual teachers stimulate pain centers to improve learning? Could a government using Pokemon Go to combat obesity keep data on your location at a given time? How will VR be used to stimulate pain and pleasure centers? Could it be used to create or cure criminal behavior?

In *A Clockwork Orange,* another of our favorite futuristic stories, the central character is a convicted murderer, addicted to violence. To cure him, scientists inject him with a medication that causes extreme nausea while he is forced to watch violent film clips.

That was a work of fiction, but could brain hacking actually be used this way? Will there be unintended side effects on the patients? Will some of the world's most violent criminals just get a quick brain hack and be set free?

What about the reverse: Can clandestine government scientists eventually erase operatives' memories and convert them into violent killing machines? Will there be a real version of the fictional Jason Bourne?

As we said, if it can be done, sooner or later it will be done. Perhaps some government or criminal organization in Russia, China, the U.S. or North Korea is working on it as you read these words.

Shel Israel grew up obsessed with science fiction books, as is reflected in this chapter. He cannot help but marvel at how many predictions of yesterday's fiction are becoming real or possible today. Some of those books had happy endings; others culminated in the destruction of humankind.

These days, scientists are even getting ahead of yesterday's writers. As we explore what could possibly go wrong, we regret that we have so many more questions than answers.

Robots at War

Among the many jobs new technologies can displace may be that of the foot soldier who, armed with weapons, faces the enemy in mortal combat. At the Pentagon, scientists are looking at ways to replace soldiers and pilots with robots and drones.

Autonomous drones can already be programmed to decide on who and where to kill—without human intervention. While that has not yet actually happened so far as the public knows, it already *can* happen, according to the Pentagon.

This has been discussed in public for some time. Another Pentagon project that has received less attention is the building of a robot infantry battalion that would replace one comprised of human soldiers.

Deputy U.S. Defense Secretary Robert Work disclosed in 2015 that Pentagon strategists were devising battle plans that would rely heavily on robots and autonomous machines to fight battles in the future.

Somehow the vision of one side using robots, and the other using humans sounds like a new form of Fourth Transformation bullying to us. We would guess that most people would root for the people and not the machines.

There are other issues as well. History shows that when one side uses technology to gain an edge, the other uses technology to offset it. When knights started using lances, the other side employed shields. When Germans introduced poison gas into warfare, the allies developed gas masks. When the countries who had developed nuclear weapons declared no one else should have them, North Korea and Iran went right ahead and defied them.

If we develop robots for war, other countries will develop them too. Then we have to imagine a battlefield sometime in the future where robots fight robots. The good news is that no one dies. Machines simply become scrap.

But the question is, who wins? And does that victory mean anything more than winning at a *Mortal Kombat* VR game? Real wars have always been decided by human deaths. It just isn't the same if one side's machines render the enemy machines inoperable.

What would happen next?

Do the people on the side of the losing robots just come out with their hands up, submitting to occupation of their lands? Will an occupying robot force then take over?

Even more frightening to us is the concept of individuals having their own machines of murder. Berkeley computer science professor Stuart Russell, in Sarah Topol's upcoming book, *Attack of the Killer Robots*, describes how some unsavory company could be making and selling personal killer drones within the next three years.

The Altered Self

At the end of the day, the ultimate concern of what could possibly go wrong is that all devices using AI can alter who we humans are as a species and as a culture.

Peter Norvig, head of Google's R&D, told us a story of just how that happened already. When the company distributed self-driving cars to employees, it warned them that they would be fired if they took their attention away from the road as the machine drove. Within days literally everyone broke the rule because the technology was so good. Watching a car drive perfectly gets so boring that we reach for our smartphones.

We don't know what the long-term impact of these technologies is on the human brain—whether it is hacked or not—and how that impact will change our perceptions of reality.

We don't know if humans will cleanse themselves of the unpleasantness of the human experience, filtering out that which pains us with entertainment and aesthetically pleasing images. We don't know what happens to compassion, or if using VR to halt pain will make us insensitive to those people and creatures who will continue to suffer pain.

We don't know if the thrill of The Void will cause heart attacks in some people, or if people engaging in social VR, as they do for hours at AltSpaceVR, will get along better or worse with real people. We don't know if Toffler's fears in *Future Shock* will be realized, that technology will cause people to become isolated.

We don't know what will happen to ethics, or if the beauty of written words will survive the transformation, or if works of art created with patience, paints and a brush will endure on canvas and frescos. We don't know if we will appreciate music as it is sung or played, or Shakespeare in its traditional words and five sequential acts.

We hope so.

We doubt very much that all these awful things we have speculated upon here will come to pass, but some will; of that we are sure.

All great progress has had significant downsides, most of them fomented by technology. Cars changed the world and yet they contribute to global warming, which could end human life forever; accidents kill tens of thousands of people in the world every year. The Internet has connected the people of the world, and today terrorists use it to recruit future murderers.

So, why should we move on? Because that's what humans do. We are the one creature on Earth that must move forward. It is in our nature. We are creatures that dream dreams and are willing to pay the price to make them come true, as T.S. Elliott observed.

And besides that, the Fourth Transformation will be so much better in so many ways than what we have ever experienced. Let's take a look at the very big upside that we see coming to most of us in the near-term future.

+++++

CHAPTER 12

Spatial Computing

"Imagination will often carry us to worlds that never were. But without it we go nowhere.

—Carl Sagan, cosmologist

We began this book with the words, "In the beginning," and that is precisely where we conclude.

In our introduction, we traced the 60-year history of computing from mainframes to the desktop where knowledge workers talked to digital devices by typing in text. Then, we described a second transformation, from text to point-and-click interfaces that allowed everyone to use computers. The third transformation was into mobile after the iPhone introduced touch interfaces, which allowed us to use digital devices everywhere.

As we write this book, we remain in the current era of mobile devices. Smartphones are central to our lives as we are sure they remain to you; most people are perfectly happy with mobile as it is.

But, as this book has endeavored to explain, the seeds of transformative change have already been planted, have germinated and are now sprouting technologies that can be used on mobile handsets, which are of course here and now, but work far better on mobile headsets, which will come soon.

This book has been all about this great migration and the devices that will transform life and work.

By definition, transformations take you from one form of existence to another. The Fourth Transformation, now unfolding, will take us from the current era of mobile into the Age of Spatial Computing where the world is our interface.

Just what does that mean and why will most people be using mixed reality headsets instead of handsets by the year 2025? Why should business strategists worry about it now, when they have ten full years before this new spatial era fully blossoms?

Because now is the time for smart business strategists to move. While 2025 may be the crossover point when everyone is using MR headsets more than phones, the earliest adopters will be walking around in them two or three years from now, we estimate.

They are not just early adopters; they are influential market makers who have greater influence over Millennials and Minecrafters than your marketing and communications teams will ever have. They shape where young adults shop, dine, watch, travel. They avoid what these influencers advise them to avoid.

As Sephora's Bridget Dolan told us in our Ubiquitous Shopping chapter, the smart brands must stay a little ahead of their customers or face obsolescence. But the world is changing so fast that there is a real possibility that tech champions will get way ahead of many brands.

Definition and History

Throughout this book, we have talked about spatial computing being the ultimate destination of the Fourth Transformation. Just what does that mean? We have described each of the earlier three transformations as going from one type of hardware into another, and in so doing they have expanded how people will use digital devices to attain greater access to whatever they want.

We have looked from the perspective of interface, evolving from punch cards, to text, to pointing and clicking, to mobile phones and touch, to mixed reality glasses that let us go wherever we want just with a movement of our eyes or perhaps a simple gesture.

And where we will go is everywhere. In this new era, the barriers of the screen disappear. We and technology are immersed together. In short, in this new era our interface is the connected world.

There's a 75-year history that starts with the science fiction masters whose fantasies are now becoming realities. The first hint of the new reality came with computer scientists in the mainframe era who shared ideas, often by typed words on white papers that they mailed to each other.

And what they dreamed of has arrived in the form of technology that we wear on our faces, technology that mixes with reality in a way that makes digital media feel physically present through interactive design, in a way that breaks down natural barriers of physics such as relationships of objects based on shape and location.

When we started this book project, such devices seemed like a sort of Holy Grail to be found somewhere in the haze of the distant future, but now they seem closer by far than we had imagined.

That is because so many well-financed companies are focusing and competing with passion and talent at being the first to arrive. These companies are innovating faster than most people thought possible and are being accepted at breathtaking speed by Millennial and Minecrafter generations.

So how do we get from where we are at this, the dawn of the Fourth Transformation, into the full sunlight of the Age of Spatial Computing?

Three Adoption Waves

We will see more digital changes in the ten-year period that started in 2016, than we have in the past 50. In terms of evolution, we are very quickly crawling out of the swamp and have started to sprout legs and lungs. Yet, by the year 2025, the amazing technologies we have talked about will be central to the everyday lives of most people: Humans will be walking fully upright and smart glasses will be the centers of their digital lives.

We see the transformation happening in three waves:

1. **Virtual reality.** This wave has already started and has probably attracted 10 million adopters in its first year. There is no end in sight. Starting in games and entertainment, spreading into education and health, more and more VR apps are coming to market and adoption will continue as far forward as we can see.

Companies that bet on VR will be in the best position to take advantage of the mixed reality world that will come quickly after.

2. **Mixed reality.** As we stated, mixed reality has far greater potential than VR and the headsets that have already arrived have generated interest and enthusiasm, but they must be refined before they become part of people's everyday lives.

   Magic Leap and Apple remain giants lurking in the shadows as we write. We expect they will have viable products available no later than 2018. With their participation, and with refined products from HoloLens and Meta, we see a second wave starting in 2018 and continuing through 2020 or so. We aren't the only ones to say this, either. Apple's CEO, Tim Cook, says that mixed reality will be far more important than VR.

3. **Smart glasses.** These are mixed reality glasses that are small, self-contained and fashionable. By 2020 or 2021, competition and Moore's Law will resolve the remaining usability and interface problems and drive end user prices down. By the end of 2021, smart glasses will be the hottest of all consumer tech categories, eclipsing smartphones in sales and, soon thereafter, in usage.

By 2025, the Fourth Transformation will be complete and billions of people all over the world will use the smart glasses as the center of their digital lives. Increasingly, they will leave their phones at home and will not miss them.

We will live in a new world. Our relationships with our devices will be far more intimate than what we have experienced with phones.

Everything. Everything.

In fact, everything, *everything* will be different and overwhelmingly so. Despite the potential for significant downsides, things will be better. Spatial computing takes humans where we have not previously gone, to ocean floors and outer space, to the living rooms of online friends in foreign countries, to battles fought years ago and to a tour of our own living hearts.

Spatial computing changes your everyday experiences, allowing you to redecorate a blank wall in your home with a different wall hanging every day, or, if you prefer, a sunny virtual window that becomes moonlit when the sun goes down.

To make it more compelling, you can have a few aliens randomly come through the window, hanging out until a family member zaps them with an eye movement, gesture or command.

On your lawn a virtual elephant or giraffe may hang out, and your kids will play tag with them.

Your work, your transportation, your health, your communication and everything else will work in ways that are wondrous compared with what we do today with the very best of our phones. What we have described in this book is just the previews of coming attractions that get this decade started.

Personalized Visions

Once again, we turned to Facebook, asking friends and followers about their visions of how life will change in the Fourth Transformation. We received a raft of thoughtful and diverse replies.

Some of our favorites:

- Kristi Hansen Onkka talked about her vision of an autonomous car with biometric sensors. When it detects a medical emergency, it becomes an autonomous emergency vehicle speeding to an emergency room and sending vital signs and medical data including warnings of allergies. It will send alerts to cars in its path so that they will automatically move out of the way.

We have talked about how robotic driving will save lives by avoiding collisions. Onkka envisions an entirely new way that autonomous cars would save lives.

- Francine Hardaway, our friend of many years, writes a blog about reinventing the aging process, called *Aging Revealed.*

  As she ages, she envisions an implant that will monitor her vital signs and medication levels, sending them continuously to a virtual doctor, an online bot. Nanotechnology will continuously send photos or video of the inside of her body for early detection of clots, cancers or orthopedic decay.

  When the inevitable time comes, her mixed reality glasses will automatically call an Uber, which will take her to a hospice of her choice where she plans to die with dignity.

- By contrast, our British friend Viv Craske looks at his young son and wonders if he will someday have to explain how daunting it was to have to actually go online, rather than just be always online. He will have to explain how people actually drove cars and why they often actually liked doing it.

  One day, he is certain he will have to explain what life without headsets had been like and what it meant to point and click. He wonders if he would have to explain that once a mouse was something you used to interact with a computer, rather than an unwanted rodent.

- Wesley Faulkner, social media manager at namecheap.com, was running for City Council in Austin, Texas, when we talked.

  He pictured attending a meeting on the other side of the world where he could not read or speak the language being used, but where his headset would translate everything he heard into English, and when he spoke, the other people would hear what he said, in real time, in their native language.

We are certain that each of these friends will get their wishes. We are the most certain for Faulkner since we are so close to what he has described already.

When Scoble visited Disneyland in Shanghai in 2016, although he spoke in English, his Disneyland hosts heard what he said in Chinese using Google Translate through their headsets.

Think of the barriers that technology will remove. Not only will we communicate in code and by using the new Visual Web, but in time the Babel of languages spoken in the world's 196 countries will no longer be a barrier in the spatial computing age.

So many barriers will be taken down, so many hard edges of society will be softened.

Gods and Soul

We have focused in this book on the flex point where technology and people interact. It was the shortest route to telling our story and why business thinkers should not just understand but adjust course.

There is more to spatial computing than just mixed reality.

IoT is the nervous system of spatial computing. As IoT continues to relentlessly expand, it will connect nearly all people to nearly all things. Each of us is becoming part of the most robust ecosystem to ever exist.

The key components of the IoT are inexpensive little sensors. They just contain a tiny bit of logic, enough to detect and report changes.

When you connect people with sensor-enabled objects all over the world, you have a global ecosystem with far greater knowledge capability than anything that has preceded it. Each of us becomes part of something far greater than ourselves, far smarter than Watson, currently the world's smartest machine.

What will that let you do? Your glasses will tell a partier which night club has the most people dancing within a ten-minute Uber ride. It will tell a fancier of Japanese food which establishment has the freshest Meguro sashimi, and it will let you know the fastest path to the nearest rest room.

If the IoT is the nervous system of Fourth Transformation technology, then artificial intelligence is its very soul.

AI allows hardware and software platforms to perform tasks as if they were human. These include visual-perception-enabled photo recognition of your favorite pet, natural language recognition such as we use when talking with Siri, and autonomous decision-making such as could be used in killer drones.

When a digital device starts to recognize your patterns so well that it can predict what you may want next, AI is making it happen.

Lately, some machine learning seems to have acquired empathy, which is why that support bot you have been speaking with seems to care so much if your problem is solved.

All these capabilities make John Markoff's book title seem so apt. AI creates *Machines of Loving Grace*.

Scoble says we are building a new God. An all-knowing one that he says will fool most people into thinking it is actually intelligent. Israel is more agnostic on the issue, and he wonders about the future of common sense. Will that autonomous car realize that the light is stuck on red and it is safe to proceed? When will Facebook stop sending him notifications on the birthdays of dead friends?

AI is also the source of what we have called the *freaky factor*. It comes from the strange feeling that these machines know things about you that you did not realize or want them to. It can be more than disconcerting, as we noted in our previous chapter. But overwhelming as this is, it is because the better machines know you, the better they can serve you.

All machines—as far as we know—are designed to serve the wishes of human masters: It is in the business interest of developers to make them do so.

It seems to us that yet another science fiction master wrote the Golden Rule for this case: Isaac Asimov's first law of robotics, which states, "A robot may not injure a human being or, through inaction, allow a human being to come to harm." Robots and intelligent machines are designed to serve and protect people—except perhaps in occasionally taking their jobs, as we discussed in the previous chapter.

The freaky factors come from the great leaps forward taken by AI in recent years. We think most people will become accustomed to such behavior and come to see the value.

For example, a couple of months before we completed this book a Tesla car experienced the first fatal crash ever while in auto pilot mode. It caused a wave of trepidation and considerable bad press and stress-filled online commentary.

But consider this: This single tragedy occurred after tens of millions of miles of autonomous car testing, and there was evidence that the human driver was not complying with safety requirements.

The reality is that autonomous cars will crash now and then, and on rare occasions there will be fatalities. But the numbers will be orders of magnitude lower than in human car crashes. Over time, the crashes will occur at intervals that are further apart because what Tesla cars learn, they share with other Teslas across the IoT, making them safer as well. Sometimes, the very stuff that makes AI freaky is the same stuff that makes it safer.

They are already far safer than human drivers. Compare that one autonomous car death in 2016 with over 30,000 deaths caused by human driving in the U.S. every year.

In fact, governments are pushing autonomous vehicles to reduce death, injury and air pollution.

The U.S. Dept. of Transportation has set guidelines to hasten adoption of autonomous vehicles on public roads by 2020. By 2025, we predict autonomous vehicles will be commonplace, if not a majority.

They are already on the road serving as taxis in Singapore. Uber is now using autonomous Ford Fusions to pick up people and goods in Pittsburgh. We're betting there will be more such projects by the time you get to read this book.

Autonomous cars are sometimes called self-driving, or robo-cars, a term industry officials dislike, because it will be a few years before a human is not required behind the wheel as a failsafe to prevent problems. But when you think about it, cars are becoming robots on wheels using AI to serve human masters, the way C-3PO served Luke in *Star Wars*, and the way digital genies serve our households while remaining stationary.

The cars are also huge, smart, connected, mobile devices, connected to everything else on the IoT as they cruise along. They are like phones, except that you sit inside them rather than hold or wear them.

Not only are automakers making them, technology companies including Apple and Google have gotten into the act as well. Uber, the ride-sharing company, says it will be the first tech company to market with driverless vehicles.

Quick Look Backwards

As we wrote this book, we got pushback from business people who are not convinced that by the year 2025 headsets will replace handsets as the primary device for most people. They pointed out that many businesses are still scrambling to catch up with the mobile devices that dominate third transformation technology.

To illustrate how tech leaders can fall from leadership to oblivion, we decided to check out the best products of 2006, the last year before the iPhone started transforming everything.

We turned to *TechCrunch*, which at that time was a new publication focused on the leading edge, and its list of best products in 2006. *TechCrunch* seemed particularly fond of the BlackBerry Pearl because it eliminated screen freeze. Other great innovations included the Xbox 360, which introduced the first interface gestures, and the iPod Shuffle 2 because it was better than playing CDs, the standard for personal music at the time.

Today, these devices are little noted and mostly forgotten. We have come so far so fast in the last ten years.

We will go much further in the next 10 years than we did in the last.

We conclude this book, aware that this story has just started. We will keep talking to you about it where and how we can. Look for us on Facebook.

You can find Robert Scoble at facebook.com/RobertScoble and Shel Israel at facebook.com/shelisrael.

And one other thing we almost forgot. Thanks for reading our book.

+++++

Links

Foreword

Introduction

Chapter 1

point cloud   https://en.wikipedia.org/wiki/Point_cloud

Ikea   https://www.youtube.com/watch?v=1S0GO5kbMYo

spatial computing   http://www.cccblog.org/2012/09/17/
                               from-gps-and-virtual-globes-to-spatial-computing-2020/

very dry white papers   https://scholar.google.com/
                               scholar?q=spatial+computing+history&hl=en&as_
                               sdt=0&as_vis=1&oi=scholart&sa=X&ved=
                               0ahUKEwivofHjycbOAhUDwGMKHeUTDlAQgQMIGjAA

Moore's Law   http://www.mooreslaw.org/

John Markoff   http://www.nytimes.com/by/john-markoff

Machines of Loving   https://www.amazon.com/Machines-
Grace   Loving-Grace-Common-Between/
                               dp/0062266683

Ambarish Mitra   https://www.crunchbase.com/person/ambarish-mitra#/
                               entity

100 times larger than   https://gigaom.com/2015/10/30/the-next-information-
today's Internet   revolution-will-be-100-times-bigger-than-the-internet/

Blippar   https://blippar.com/en/

most business growth   http://monitor.icef.com/2014/03/
                               the-role-of-emerging-markets-in-shaping-global-demand/

Immanuel Kant   https://en.wikipedia.org/wiki/Democratic_peace_theory

Gary Vaynerchuck   https://twitter.com/garyvee

GoPro Hero 4   https://shop.gopro.com/hero4/hero4-black/CHDHX-401.
                               html

Cube 360   http://actioncamadvisor.com/
                               cube-360-action-camera-360-degree-price/

| Eric Romo | http://www.forbes.com/sites/joshwolfe/2015/01/11/rocket-scientist-launches-into-virtual-worlds/#49084d8413de |
| AltspaceVR | http://altvr.com |

Chapter 2

Marshall McLuhan	https://en.wikipedia.org/wiki/Marshall_McLuhan
Head-Mounted Displays	https://en.wikipedia.org/wiki/Head-mounted_display
Groundswell	https://www.amazon.com/dp/B004XOZ7K2/ref=dp-kindle-redirect?_encoding=UTF8&btkr=1
gamer is 31	http://venturebeat.com/2014/04/29/gaming-advocacy-group-the-average-gamer-is-31-and-most-play-on-a-console/
Microsoft Xbox	https://en.wikipedia.org/wiki/Xbox
Sony PlayStation	https://en.wikipedia.org/wiki/PlayStation
Nvidia	http://www.nvidia.com/content/global/global.php
best possible smartphone	http://www.huffingtonpost.com/2013/03/01/millennials-car-ownership_n_2789454.html
sold 15,000 headsets in its first ten minutes	http://venturebeat.com/2016/02/29/htc-sold-15000-800-vive-virtual-reality-headsets-in-10-minutes/
1.2 billion	http://venturebeat.com/2013/11/25/more-than-1-2-billion-people-are-playing-games/
average of two players	http://www.theesa.com/wp-content/uploads/2015/04/ESA-Essential-Facts-2015.pdf
with a majority going for 1976	https://en.wikipedia.org/wiki/Millennials

Sparks and Honey	http://www.sparksandhoney.com/
Lethal Generosity	http://www.amazon.com/Lethal-Generosity-Shel-Israel/dp/1517365899
naturally acquiring versus consciously learning languages	http://en.wikipedia.org/wiki/Second_language
that is what scientists say	http://accenteraser.com/blog/5-myths-about-why-you-have-an-accent/
back to Rome	http://www.albany.edu/~sw7656/
Hopscotch	https://www.gethopscotch.com/
teaches children to code	https://itunes.apple.com/us/app/hopscotch-coding-for-kids/id617098629?mt=8&ign-mpt=uo%3D4
best-selling PC video game	https://en.wikipedia.org/wiki/List_of_best-selling_PC_games
Gamespot estimated	http://www.gamespot.com/articles/minecraft-passes-100-million-registered-users-14-3-million-sales-on-pc/1100-6417972/
Markus Persson	https://en.wikipedia.org/wiki/Markus_Persson
15 takers	http://www.wired.com/2013/11/minecraft-book/
over 150 million uploads	https://www.youtube.com/results?search_query=Minecraft
Wired magazine	http://www.wired.com/2013/11/minecraft-book/

Microsoft's own Hololens	http://www.engadget.com/2015/07/08/ minecraft-hololens-minecon/

Chapter 3

The Twilight Zone	https://www.youtube.com/playlist?list= PLYkG4AyFVMHK4d9VDUH1EwaMrYaAHl3jy
recently invented	http://www.economist.com/node/883706
the primary rule	http://classics.mit.edu/Aristotle/poetics.1.1.html
Shari Frilot	http://www.essence.com/2016/01/21/how-sundance- programmer-shari-frilot-keeps-film-festival-diverse
Sundance Film Festival	http://www.sundance.org/festivals/sundance-film-festival
Dear Angelica	https://www.oculus.com/en-us/blog/oculus-story-studio- previews-dear-angelica-at-sundance-2016/
Oculus Story Studio	https://storystudio.oculus.com/en-us/
The Verge	http://www.theverge.com/2016/1/26/10833340/ dear-angelica-quill-oculus-story-studio-sundance-2016
Adi Robertson	http://www.theverge.com/2012/7/31/3172903/ verge-favorites-adi-robertson
Ted Schilowitz	https://www.linkedin.com/in/ted-schilowitz-a084233
Wild	https://en.wikipedia.org/wiki/Wild_(2014_film)
Penrose	http://www.penrosestudios.com/
Eugene Chung	http://me.eugenechung.co/
The Rose and I	https://www.buzzfeed.com/brendanklinkenberg/ the-beautiful-the-rose-and-i-may-be-the-best-argument- for-vi?utm_term=.cyrx5qD8l#.psbJopkqw

Allumette	http://www.penrosestudios.com/stories/2016/4/13/introducing-allumette
The Curious Incident of the Dog in the Night Time	http://curiousonbroadway.com/
Sleep No More	https://en.wikipedia.org/wiki/Sleep_No_More_(2011_play)
Environmental Theaters	http://www.britannica.com/art/environmental-theatre
The Lion King	http://www.lionking.com/
Circle of Life	https://www.youtube.com/watch?v=GibiNy4d4gc
Total Cinema 360	http://totalcinema360.com/
Minskoff Theater	http://minskofftheatre.com/
Andrew Flatt	https://www.linkedin.com/in/andrew-flatt-a329663
Jaunt	http://recode.net/2015/09/21/jaunts-new-65-million-round-makes-it-highest-funded-virtual-reality-startup-so-far/
Walt Disney Imagineering (WDI)	http://wdi.disneycareers.com/en/default/
everything that Disney builds	http://fortune.com/2015/08/13/disney-imagineering-vr/
Mark Mine	http://www.fmx.de/program2015/speaker/1373
Shanghai Disneyland	https://www.shanghaidisneyresort.com/en/
Avatar Land	http://www.slashfilm.com/avatar-land-d23-expo-2015/
Star Wars	http://collider.com/star-wars-land-concept-art-disney/
Universal Studios	http://variety.com/2015/digital/news/landmark-entertainment-looks-to-launch-virtual-reality-theme-parks-1201514371/

to vomit	http://www.vrfocus.com/2014/09/vr-park-launches-steam-greenlight-campaign/
Six Flags Magic Mountain has added VR headsets	http://www.cosmicbooknews.com/content/superman-virtual-reality-coasters-coming-fix-flags#axzz428mxSacX
virtual dugout	http://www.usnews.com/news/sports/articles/2016-04-08/red-sox-to-offer-fans-virtual-reality-experience-at-fenway
The Void	https://thevoid.com/
Curtis Hickman	https://www.linkedin.com/in/curtis-hickman-250b40a
he previewed them at the TED conference	http://blog.ted.com/the-future-of-virtual-reality-will-literally-spray-you-in-the-face/
Ghostbusters Dimension	https://thevoid.com/dimensions/ghostbusters
Madame Tussauds New York	https://www.madametussauds.com/new-york/en/
Subpac vest	http://www.wgrz.com/news/feeling-the-beat-mitchells-story/301451247
NFL took in $12 billion. But the stadium competes, not only with	http://money.cnn.com/2015/07/20/news/green-bay-packers-revenue/
drone racing	https://www.facebook.com/quartznews/videos/1098586363508398/?__mref=message
sitting atop	https://www.youtube.com/watch?v=UlFpsJ_vzfI
Formula One	https://en.wikipedia.org/wiki/Formula_One_racing
Steve Ross, owner of the Miami Dolphins	http://www.theverge.com/2015/8/12/9136279/drone-racing-league-one-million-backing
Sun Life Stadium	http://www.newmiamistadium.com/

AltSpaceVR	http://altvr.com/
Eric Romo	https://www.linkedin.com/in/eric-romo-79ba641
Bruce Wooden	https://www.linkedin.com/in/brucewooden
a new, fully tracked wireless headset	http://arstechnica.com/gaming/2016/10/oculus-working-on-wireless-headset-with-inside-out-tracking/
According to Business Insider	http://www.businessinsider.com/virtual-reality-headset-sales-explode-2015-4
bigger than the TV industry in its first five years	http://www.businessinsider.com/goldman-sachs-predicts-vr-will-be-bigger-than-tv-in-10-years-2016-1

Chapter 4

AR will go mainstream on phones	https://techcrunch.com/2016/07/28/pokemon-not-magic-leap/
1996 when it introduced Pokemon	http://bulbapedia.bulbagarden.net/wiki/History_of_Pok%C3%A9mon
Niantic Labs	https://www.nianticlabs.com/
downloaded over 75 million times	http://www.usatoday.com/story/tech/gaming/2016/07/26/pokmon-go-downloads-top-75-million/87575470/
43 minutes daily, more than Instagram, WhatsApp or Snapchat	https://www.similarweb.com/blog/pokemon-go
Pokestops	http://www.ign.com/wikis/pokemon-go/PokeStops
Snapchat	https://www.snapchat.com/
$20 billion	http://www.investopedia.com/articles/markets/081415/startup-analysis-how-much-snapchat-worth.asp

overtaken Facebook in popularity	http://www.businessinsider.com/ snapchat-overshadows-publisher-and-brand-content-2016-5
60 percent of US smartphone users	http://www.latimes.com/business/technology/la-fi-tn-snapchat-olympics-20160429-snap-story.html
fastest growing social network	http://www.globalwebindex.net/blog/ snapchat-was-the-fastest-growing-social-app-of-2014
Lenses	https://support.snapchat.com/en-US/ca/lenses
Pinpoint Marketing	http://shelisrael.com/3275-2/
Brian Fanzo	https://www.linkedin.com/in/brianfanzo
Gary Vaynerchuk	https://www.garyvaynerchuk.com/ the-snap-generation-a-guide-to-snapchats-history/
Business Insider	http://www.businessinsider.com/
Vergence Labs	https://techcrunch.com/2014/12/16/ snapchat-emails-not-so-ephemeral/
Obvious Engineering	https://techcrunch.com/2016/06/03/snapchat-secretly-acquires-seene-a-computer-vision-startup-that-lets-mobile-users-make-3d-selfies/
Osterhout Design Group (ODG)	http://www.osterhoutgroup.com/home
Nima Shams	https://events.bizzabo.com/awe2016/agenda/ speakers/122049
told us	https://www.facebook.com/RobertScoble/videos/ vb.501319654/10153812695049655/?type=2&theater&notif_t=comment_mention
BMW	https://www.youtube.com/watch?v=-m7B-91KBXg
visually impaired due to macular degeneration	https://www.fastcompany.com/3057360/ how-odgs-smart-glasses-can-help-the-visually-impaired

Atheer Air	http://www.atheerair.com/shop
10 AR headset brands	http://www.hongkiat.com/blog/augmented-reality-smart-glasses/

Chapter 5

Edward Albee	http://www.biography.com/people/edward-albee-9178576
Meron Gribetz	https://www.google.com/#q=Meron+Gribetz
to call up a colleague	https://www.ted.com/talks/meron_gribetz_a_glimpse_of_the_future_through_an_augmented_reality_headset?language=en
Alex Kipman	http://www.businessinsider.com/microsoft-alex-kipman-hololens-kinect-2015-1
Trimble Architecture	https://trimble.squarespace.com/
Case Western Reserve University	http://case.edu/hololens/
Volvo	http://www.geekwire.com/2015/volvo-to-launch-virtual-showroom-using-microsofts-hololens-sometime-next-year/
Saab	http://saabgroup.com/media/news-press/news/2016-03/saab-and-microsoft-hololens-working-to-redefine-the-training-and-education-experience/
Lowe's	http://www.geekwire.com/2016/microsoft-brings-hololens-lowes-kitchen-renovation-previews/
Chris Capossela	https://news.microsoft.com/exec/chris-capossela/#sm.0014emim6drif8z11td1qipjrwz0m
declared in April 2016	http://www.geekwire.com/2016/microsoft-marketing-chief-hololens-totally-underestimated-commercial-interest/
Soren Harner	https://www.linkedin.com/in/sharner

world's largest personal computer maker	https://en.wikipedia.org/wiki/Lenovo
Tencent	https://en.wikipedia.org/wiki/Tencent
Loook.io	http://www.loook.io/
over $200 billion	http://www.marketwatch.com/story/apple-isnt-really-sitting-on-216-billion-in-cash-2016-01-26
United Kingdom	https://en.wikipedia.org/wiki/List_of_countries_by_foreign-exchange_reserves

Chapter 6

Eyefluence	http://eyefluence.com/
eye-tracking	https://en.wikipedia.org/wiki/Eye_tracking
brains process what they see as fast as the eye sees it	http://repository.cmu.edu/cgi/viewcontent.cgi?article=1731&context=psychology
quadriplegics to manipulate objects	http://www.medgadget.com/2012/07/ultra-cheap-3d-eye-tracking-for-quadriplegics-and-other-seriously-disabled-patients-video.html
Stephen Hawking's speech synthesis system	http://www.businessinsider.com/an-eye-tracking-interface-helps-als-patients-use-computers-2015-9
Fove	http://www.getfove.com/
Eye Interaction	http://eyefluence.com/what-we-do/
Whac-a-Mole	https://en.wikipedia.org/wiki/Whac-A-Mole

Intelligent Agents   http://www.mind.ilstu.edu/curriculum/ants_nasa/
                              intelligent_agents.php

Part 2

Thomas Jefferson   http://www.huffingtonpost.com/jess-coleman/every-
                             generation-needs-a-_b_1067149.html

Chapter 7

Bridget Dolan   https://www.linkedin.com/in/bridget-dolan-75a9b41

Sephora Innovation   http://www.fastcompany.
Labs   com/3043166/most-creative-people/
                             first-look-inside-sephoras-new-innovation-lab

with a digital billboard   https://www.youtube.com/watch?v=l8Y5MDVhZDQ

Google Daydream   http://www.techradar.com/news/phone-
                             and-communications/mobile-phones/
                             android-vr-release-date-news-features-1321245

launched Daydream   http://variety.com/2016/digital/news/
View, a new VR   google-daydream-headset-79-dollars-1201876438/
headset

autonomous cars   https://www.google.com/selfdrivingcar/

Verne   http://www.theverge.com/2016/8/3/12369460/
                             google-maps-himalayas-android-app-game

$30 trillion chunk   http://www.mckinsey.com/global-themes/winning-in-
                             emerging-markets/winning-the-30-trillion-decathlon-how-
                             to-succeed-in-emerging-markets

Phab 2 Pro	http://shop.lenovo.com/us/en/ tango/?gclid=Cj0KEQjwlNy8BRC676-W0JezxbwBEiQ A4Ydg0dL1Qkqggzjt102gn73wBg2rwpIjhpM0vvfr_9fa ADQaArpC8P8HAQ&cid=us:sem%7Cse%7Cgoogle%7 CAll_Products%7CNX_Lenovo_All_Products_DSA&ef_ id=VMGx0QAAAeVVS1YA:20160726150212:s
Johnny Lee	https://www.linkedin.com/in/johnnychunglee
Dolby stereoscopic	http://blog.lenovo.com/en/blog/behind-the-lenovo-phab-2-pro-the-worlds-first-tango-enabled-smartphone/
Larry Yang	https://www.linkedin.com/in/lryang
Kyle Nel	https://www.linkedin.com/in/kylenel
Lowe's Innovation Labs	http://www.lowesinnovationlabs.com/#about
recognized thought leader	https://www.youtube.com/watch?v=k8tg-eL8Y68
OSHbots	https://www.youtube.com/watch?v=Sp9176vm7Co
Holoroom	http://www.lowesinnovationlabs.com/holoroom/
Star Trek	https://en.wikipedia.org/wiki/Holodeck
Aisle411	http://aisle411.com/
Nathan Pettyjohn	https://www.linkedin.com/in/nathan-pettyjohn-17619710
Eric Johnsen	https://www.linkedin.com/in/ejohnsen
$382 billion global industry	http://www.forbes.com/pictures/lmj45jdlf/ top-10-global-beauty-brands/#8c8f2c5ef447
L'Oreal	http://www.lorealparisusa.com/en/beauty-magazine/ makeup/makeup-looks/makeupgenius-changes-makeup-application-forever.aspx
Taaz	http://www.taaz.com/virtual-makeover

Sally Beauty	http://www.sallybeauty.com/makeover/virtual-makeover,default,pg.html
Sephora	http://seph.me/2dDnG8a
over 11 million clips	https://www.youtube.com/results?search_query=Beauty+tips
Beauty Talk	http://community.sephora.com/
Myers	http://www.myer.com.au/
first personal department store	https://www.youtube.com/watch?v=yAuiXhJPnr8&feature=youtu.be
Vanessa Whiteside	http://www.huffingtonpost.co.uk/author/vanessa-whiteside
a vision piece in	http://www.huffingtonpost.co.uk/vanessa-whiteside/virtual-reality-retail_b_9608504.html
virtual reality	http://www.bloomberg.com/news/articles/2016-08-24/best-buy-poised-to-be-virtual-reality-s-first-mainstream-test

Chapter 8

Aldous Huxley	http://www.biography.com/people/aldous-huxley-9348198
Tom Mainelli	http://www.recode.net/authors/Tom%20Mainelli
wrote in Recode	http://www.recode.net/2016/2/1/11587458/the-augmented-reality-enterprise-opportunity
was 30 percent faster and 90 percent more accurate	http://www.pwc.com/us/en/technology-forecast/augmented-reality/augmented-reality-road-ahead.html
Daqri Smart Helmet	http://daqri.com/home/product/daqri-smart-helmet/
STRIVR Labs	http://www.strivrlabs.com/

a $100 million program	http://www.cnn.com/2016/09/14/health/nfl-concussion-safety-initiative/
4500 players who had suffered head injuries	http://www.si.com/nfl/2016/09/29/nfl-concussion-lawsuit-appeal-supreme-court
view what his life as a Warrior	http://www.usatoday.com/story/sports/nba/warriors/2016/07/07/kevin-durant-chemistry-culture-free-agency-golden-state-warriors/86827976/
NextVR	http://www.nextvr.com/
Mercedes has been using smart glasses	http://www.wassom.com/international-summit-on-augmented-reality-in-the-automotive-industry-part-2-ar-in-industrial-processes.html
makes 3D glasses standard equipment	http:/www.engadget.com/2015/11/24/volkswagen-is-issuing-ar-glasses-as-standard-factory-equipment
display information	https://www.engadget.com/2014/08/19/myo-armband-smart-glasses-enterprise-solutions/
virtual showrooms	http://dealervideoshowroom.com/
in all processes	https://www.youtube.com/watch?v=VGtCQWROytw
safety inspections and repair instruction	https://www.youtube.com/watch?v=S8jMgBimuxg
for employee and customer training	http://www.thonline.com/news/video_ceab3990-eab8-11e4-b3b7-07344067425b.html
Dr. Keith Bujack	https://www.facebook.com/RobertScoble/videos/10153852305869655/?__mref=message
Space Station repairs	http://www.popsci.com/astronauts-start-using-hololens-on-space-station
black-and-white film	https://www.youtube.com/watch?v=RMINSD7MmT4
Skanska USA	http://www.skanska.com/

Studio 216	http://www.studio216.com/
midst of a major project	http://www.digitaltrends.com/virtual-reality/studio216-hololens-seattle/
According to Techcrunch	https://techcrunch.com/2016/02/22/virtual-reality-in-the-enterprise/
Floored, Inc.	http://www.floored.com/
Construction Week Online	http:/www.constructionweekonline.com/article-38227-augmented-reality-and-virtual-reality-in-fm/
Sotheby's International Realty	http://fortune.com/2015/09/09/virtual-reality-real-estate/

Chapter 9

Fear	https://www.amazon.com/Fear-Jeff-Abbott-ebook/dp/B00AMILB30/ref=sr_1_1?s=books&ie=UTF8&qid=1476134589&sr=1-1&keywords=fear+jeff+abbott
topped $3 trillion	http://www.nytimes.com/2015/12/03/us/politics/health-spending-in-us-topped-3-trillion-last-year.html?_r=0
Mindmaze	http://www.mindmaze.ch/
Tej Tadi	https://www.linkedin.com/in/tejtadi
valued at over $1 billion	http://www.forbes.com/sites/aarontilley/2016/02/17/mindmaze-raises-100-million-at-a-1-billion-valuation-for-neural-virtual-reality/#3b6eb9a87557
motion capture	https://en.wikipedia.org/wiki/Motion_capture
phantom pain	https://en.wikipedia.org/wiki/Phantom_pain
15 million stroke victims worldwide	http://www.strokecenter.org/patients/about-stroke/stroke-statistics/

NeuroGoggles

http://www.psfk.com/2015/03/neurogoggles-mindmaze-mindleap-virtual-reality-gaming.html

flames shoot from his fingers

https://www.youtube.com/watch?v=NoXhfHFeyPE

About 1.1 percent of the world's population

http://www.schizophrenia.com/szfacts.htm

$100 billion annually

http://www.ncbi.nlm.nih.gov/pubmed/26937191

VR headsets for children

http://www.sfchronicle.com/health/article/For-children-in-pain-virtual-reality-offers-9176380.php?t=e8d2c11cb600af33be&cmpid=fb-premium

children suffering from cancer

https://www.tnooz.com/article/expedia-helps-some-ill-children-travel-with-virtual-reality-video

Braingate

http://www.braingate.org/

the first bionic man

http://www.ric.org/research/accomplishments/Bionic/

pour liquid from a bottle into a glass

http://www.nytimes.com/2016/04/14/health/paralysis-limb-reanimation-brain-chip.html?emc=edit_na_20160413&nlid=35299517&ref=headline&_r=1

5.6 million

http://www.techinsider.io/we-are-in-the-age-of-the-brain-implant-2016-4

1.9 million

http://www.newsmax.com/Health/Health-Wire/quadriplegics-life-span-life-expectancy-injury/2014/03/30/id/562522/

neurotechnology

https://en.wikipedia.org/wiki/Neurotechnology

Swiss Federal Institute of Technology of Zurich

http://www.topuniversities.com/universities/eth-zurich-swiss-federal-institute-technology

world's first Cyborg Olympics

http://thenextweb.com/insider/2016/03/29/worlds-first-cyborg-olympics-coming/#gref

Ekso Bionics	http://eksobionics.com/product/ekso-bionics-ekso-gt/
eight spinal cord injury victims were able to move limbs and feel sensations	https://www.newscientist.com/article/2100780-virtual-reality-helps-eight-paralysed-people-feel-their-legs/
Miguel Nicolelis	http://www.nicolelislab.net/
Genworth Aging Experience	http://www.reuters.com/article/ us-usa-elderly-idUSKCN0X32BF
tinnitus	https://en.wikipedia.org/wiki/Tinnitus
a museum staff member	http://www.reuters.com/article/ us-usa-elderly-idUSKCN0X32BF
pelvic osteosarcoma	http://www.ncbi.nlm.nih.gov/pmc/articles/PMC2628496/
Timothy Rapp	http://nyulangone.org/doctors/1619941945/timothy-b-rapp
Pierre Saadeh	http://nyulangone.org/doctors/1760404933/pierre-b-saadeh
NYU Langone Medical Center	http://nyulangone.org/
fill the hole left by the cancer with bone shavings, and thus save use of the leg	https://backchannel.com/augmented-reality-just-saved-this-patient-s-leg-so-why-aren-t-more-surgeons-using-it-7d6d4b653e0f#.svjyax1zi
Dassault Systemes	http://www.fastcodesign.com/3058332/exploring-this-huge-virtual-heart-showed-me-the-future-of-medicine
software design corporation	http://www.3ds.com/
Simulia Living Heart Project	http://www.3ds.com/products-services/simulia/solutions/ life-sciences/living-heart-human-model/
toured the virtual heart	https://www.fastcodesign.com/3058332/exploring-this-huge-virtual-heart-showed-me-the-future-of-medicine

285 million blind people	http://www.who.int/mediacentre/factsheets/fs282/en/
NuEyes	http://www.bloomberg.com/news/articles/2016-06-02/nueyes-visionary-design-helps-restore-sight
SecondSight	http://www.secondsight.com/
HoloHear	https://www.youtube.com/watch?v=mCNsN01F1AA
run the app	https://www.facebook.com/RobertScoble/videos/pcb.10154245558709655/10154245513894655/?type=3&theater
Amber Murray	https://www.linkedin.com/in/amberrmurray
360 million people	http://www.who.int/mediacentre/factsheets/fs300/en/
to safely cross a busy street	http://www.disabled-world.com/assistivedevices/computer/vr-tech.php
an AR system to encourage autistic children	https://www.cl.cam.ac.uk/~zb223/pub/bai_IEEE_TVCG_manualscript.pdf
Autism Speaks	https://science.grants.autismspeaks.org/search/grants/neural-basis-response-virtual-reality-social-cognition-training-adults-asd

Chapter 10

Harry Edwards	http://www.blackpast.org/aah/harry-edwards-1942
Case Western Reserve University	http://case.edu/hololens/
Cleveland Clinic	http://my.clevelandclinic.org/
Microsoft Build	https://build.microsoft.com/
Prof. Pamela B. Davis	https://case.edu/medicine/meet-the-dean/deans-bio/

demo then showed most of what is	http://case.edu/hololens/
Saab is training future sea captains	https://www.facebook.com/photo.php?fbid=10154219560939655&set=a.10150326718589655.360975.501319654&type=3&theater
Google Expeditions	https://www.google.com/edu/expeditions/#explore
Alchemy VR	http://www.alchemyvr.com/alchemy-vr-and-google-bring-virtual-reality-to-classrooms-around-the-world/
Buckingham Palace	https://www.royalcollection.org.uk/learning/resource/virtual-reality-tour-buckingham-palace
VR ViewMaster	http://bit.ly/2enVY3x
Nearpod	https://nearpod.com/
Salesforce CEO Mark Benioff	https://en.wikipedia.org/wiki/Marc_Benioff
tours of global current and past wonders	http://fortune.com/2016/02/25/school-districts-teaching-through-virtual-reality
Apollo 11 flight to the moon	http://immersivevreducation.com/
Unity Vision Award	https://unity3d.com/news/vision-vrar-awards-2016-finalists-announced
zSpace	http://zspace.com/
Books & Magic	http://booksandmagic.com/
The Little Mermaid	http://booksandmagic.com/
Arloon Chemistry	https://www.youtube.com/watch?v=DXLyBQTS5-w
NetDragon	http://www.netdragon.com/

bigger market in educating kids	http://www.bloomberg.com/news/articles/2016-08-09/ virtual-reality-classrooms-another-way-chinese-kids-gain-an-edge
British online education provider Promethean World	https://www.prometheanworld.com/news-events/news/ netdragon-expands-globally-with-the-completion-of-promethean-acquisition
Singularity Hub	http://singularityhub.com/
Jason Gantz observed	http://singularityhub.com/.../the-virtual-reality.../

Chapter 11

Isaac Asimov	http://www.asimovonline.com/asimov_home_page.html
Fashionistas	http://www.urbandictionary.com/define. php?term=fashionista
Watson	http://www.ibm.com/watson/what-is-watson.html
Machines of Loving Grace	https://www.amazon.com/Machines-Loving-Grace-Common-Between/ dp/0062266683
Childhood's End	http://amzn.to/2eLfrcj
birth rate is below the replacement rate	http://www.japantimes.co.jp/community/2016/02/10/ voices/japan-birth-rate-beginning-end-just-new-beginning/#.V_qHR5MrKA8
economy is faltering	https://www.weforum.org/agenda/2016/02/japans-population-is-shrinking-what-does-it-mean-for-the-economy/
Martin Varsavsky	https://en.wikipedia.org/wiki/Mart%C3%ADn_Varsavsky
Brave New World	https://www.amazon.com/dp/B00JTYQJ3K/ ref=dp-kindle-redirect?_encoding=UTF8&btkr=1

feelies	http://study.com/academy/lesson/feelies-in-brave-new-world.html
Roger McNamee	https://www.facebook.com/chubbywombat?fref=ufi
Deirdre Porter	https://www.facebook.com/deirdre.porter?fref=ufi
Orson Welles	https://en.wikipedia.org/wiki/Orson_Welles
H. G. Wells	http://www.biography.com/people/hg-wells-39224
War of the Worlds	https://en.wikipedia.org/wiki/The_War_of_the_Worlds_(radio_drama)
Keitchi Matsuda	http://km.cx/about/
confetti of sales messages	https://vimeo.com/8569187
with notifications and offers	https://hypebeast.com/2016/5/hyper-reality-short-film
Irena Cronin	https://www.facebook.com/irena.cronin
VR Society	http://uploadvr.com/vr-society-launches/
Rob Thompson	https://www.facebook.com/robthompsonagent?fref=ufi&pnref=story
children fleeing their village after it was hit by napalm	http://www.businessinsider.com/facebook-lifts-ban-on-napalm-girl-vietnam-war-photo-2016-9
spray someone seated on a $4,000 My Satis	http://www.forbes.com/sites/kashmirhill/2013/08/15/heres-what-it-looks-like-when-a-smart-toilet-gets-hacked-video/#30adcfc12b15
ransomware	https://www.microsoft.com/en-us/security/portal/mmpc/shared/ransomware.aspx
tamper with the 2016 election	http://www.cbsnews.com/news/how-russian-hackers-could-disrupt-the-u-s-election/

Brain hacking http://www.businessinsider.com/brain-hacking-will-make-us-smarter-and-more-productive-2014-7

controlled electric jolts http://www.npr.org/sections/
to the cranium health-shots/2014/05/19/312479753/
hacking-the-brain-with-electricity-dont-try-this-at-home

chip implants http://bigthink.com/
dangerous-ideas/32-implant-memory-chips-in-our-brains

A Clockwork Orange https://en.wikipedia.org/wiki/A_Clockwork_Orange

Robert Work http://www.washingtontimes.com/topics/robert-work/

robots and http://www.washingtontimes.com/news/2015/apr/8/
autonomous machines inside-the-ring-pentagon-prepares-robots-to-fight-/
to fight battles

personal killer drones http://kottke.org/16/08/
our-tiny-autonomous-killer-drone-future

Chapter 12

Carl Sagan http://www.carlsagan.com/

Kristi Hansen Onkka https://www.facebook.com/kristi.hansen.716?fref=ufi

Francine Hardaway https://www.facebook.com/francine.hardaway?fref=ufi

Aging Revealed https://medium.com/@hardaway

Viv Craske https://www.facebook.com/vivcraske1?fref=ufi

Wesley Faulkner https://www.linkedin.com/in/wesley83

world's 196 countries http://www.infoplease.com/ipa/A0932875.html

first law of robotics https://en.wikipedia.org/wiki/Three_Laws_of_Robotics

first fatal crash http://www.nytimes.com/2016/07/13/business/tesla-autopilot-fatal-crash-investigation.html?_r=0

has set guidelines to hasten adoption	http://www.techrepublic.com/article/us-dot-unveils-worlds-first-autonomous-vehicle-policy-ushering-in-age-of-driverless-cars/
taxis in Singapore	https://www.bloomberg.com/news/articles/2016-08-25/world-s-first-self-driving-taxis-debut-in-singapore
Uber is now using autonomous Ford Fusions	https://techcrunch.com/2016/09/14/1386711/
best products in 2006	https://techcrunch.com/2006/12/05/crunchgears-best-of-2006/
facebook.com/ RobertScoble	https://www.facebook.com/RobertScoble
facebook.com/ shelisrael	http://www.facebook.com/shelisrael

Glossary

[A]

Artificial empathy describes the characteristic of artificial intelligence that recognizes human social signals, such as visual data, and responds in a way that appears to be human.

Amazon Echo is a household device from Amazon that uses natural language and artificial intelligence to speak with people nearby, through Alexis, a female personality. It can manage a digital home and even tell jokes. It is an example of a digital genie — our term for a device that fulfills wishes for those who use them.

Artificial intelligence (AI) is the simulation of intelligence exhibited by digital machines or software. It is also the of study of how to create computers, digital devices and software capable of intelligent behavior.

Augmented reality (AR) is a live direct or indirect view of a physical, real-world environment whose elements are supplemented by computer-generated sensory input such as sound, video, graphics or location data.

Autonomous car is a vehicle capable of sensing its environment and navigating without human input.

[B]

Brain hacking is a method of manipulating or interfering with the structure and/or function of neurons for improvement or repair in the brain or central nervous system.

[D]

The **Darwin Awards** are a set of tongue-in-cheek annual prizes given to individuals who have supposedly contributed to human evolution by removing themselves from the gene pool because their own stupid actions led to their death or sterilization.

Demographers seek to understand population dynamics by investigating birth, migration and aging. All three contribute to changes in populations, including how people inhabit the earth, form societies, develop culture, make purchases and share information.

Digital genies is our term for artificially intelligent devices such as Amazon Echo that fulfill "wishes" they receive in the form of voice commands.

Digital divide refers to the demographic or geographic gap between people who have access to modern information and communications technology and those who do not.

[E]

Eye tracking is the process of measuring either the point of gaze or the motion of an eye relative to the head. An **eye tracker** is a device for measuring eye positions and eye movement. They are used in research on the visual system, in psychology, in psycholinguistics, in marketing, as an input method for human-computer interaction and in product design. Eye tracking differs from eye interaction, the feature that allows users to open, move, or manipulate virtual objects by just moving their eyes.

[F]

First-person view (FPV), also known as remote-person view (RPV), or simply video piloting, is a method used to control a radio-operated vehicle from the driver or pilot's viewpoint. It is used to remotely pilot a radio-controlled aircraft or other type of unmanned aerial vehicle (UAV). The first-person perspective comes from an onboard camera, fed wirelessly as video to a digital headset or a video monitor worn by the operator.

[G]

Generation Z, often shortened to Gen Z, refers to people born later than the Millennials. This generation is also known as iGeneration, Homeland Generation, or Plurals. The generation is loosely defined as those with birth years starting in the mid-1990s and continuing to today. A significant aspect of this generation is its widespread use of the internet from preschool years. In this book, we describe this group as the Minecraft Generation, or Minecrafters, after the popular game that has taught millions of them to code and share across geographical boundaries.

Geofilters are augmented reality overlays defined by location and time. They are best known for their uses in Snapchat but are used by many other social marketing technologies as well, including Aisle411.

A **GUI**, or graphical user interface, is an interface that allows users to interact with electronic devices through graphical icons and visual indicators, as opposed to text-based user interfaces that use typed commands or menus.

[H]

A **head-mounted display** (HMD) is a display device, worn on the head or as part of a helmet, that has a small display in front of one or both eyes. All digital headsets are HMDs.

[I]

An **intelligent agent (IA)** is a software agent capable of making decisions on behalf of users. Intelligent agents learn from each task they perform, thus becoming smarter over time, and eventually understanding user patterns so well that they can anticipate requests before users actually make them.

The **Internet of Things (IoT)** is the rapidly expanding network of physical objects such as devices, vehicles, buildings and other objects that contain embedded electronics, software, sensors and network connectivity. This enables things to collect and exchange data. The IoT is the bloodstream of the Fourth Transformation and the coming age of spatial computing.

[L]

Lethal Generosity is a 2015 book by Shel Israel. Written as a follow-up to *Age of Context*, it explains how the fundamental convergence of mobile, data, social media, the IoT and location technologies is changing online and in-store retail experiences.

[M]

Magic Leap is a US startup working on an advanced mixed reality headset reputed to feature the first virtual retinal display. It will superimpose 3D computer-generated imagery over real-world objects by projecting a digital light field into the user's eye.

Herbert Marshall McLuhan (July 21, 1911—December 31, 1980) was a Canadian English professor, a communications theory philosopher and public intellectual. His work is viewed as one of the cornerstones of media theory. It continues to have practical applications in the advertising and television industries.

Med tech is technology used for medical purposes.

The **Minecraft Generation** is our term to describe the generation that follows Millennials. Often referred to by traditional demographers as Gen Z, this generation is the second generation of digital natives.

Minecrafters is short for the Minecraft Generation.

Mixed reality (MR) is the merging of real and virtual worlds to produce new environments and visualizations where physical and digital objects co-exist and interact in real time. It is similar to augmented reality because it integrates computer-generated images together with images of what is really there, but MR integrates them so tightly that users cannot tell the difference between what is real and what is virtual.

Motion capture is the process of recording the movement of objects or people and reusing it digitally. It is used in military, entertainment, sports, medicine, computer vision and robotics. In filmmaking and video games, it refers to recording the actions of human actors and using their recorded motion in digital character animations. Med tech developers use it to trick the brain in ways that reduce pain and bypass broken nervous systems.

[N]

NeuroGoggles is MindMaze's proprietary medical gamer headset. It operates on a unique neurotechnology engine that allows players to move virtual objects by brain command faster than any other method. When it is combined with a wearable mesh containing 32 electrodes, fitted over the brain, it becomes a medical device.

Neurotechnology is any technology that influences how people understand the brain and various aspects of consciousness and thought. In this book, it refers to technologies that are designed to improve and repair brain functions.

[O]

Oculus Story Studio is an organization made up of a small film and game developers dedicated to exploring "immersive cinema."

Omnichannel refers to a multichannel approach to sales that seeks to provide the customer with a seamless shopping experience.

[P]

Paradigm shifts are fundamental changes that alter basic societal behavior, such as the move from mainframes to desktop computers, from desktops to mobile, or from mobile to head-mounted devices.

PlayStation is a series of video game consoles created and developed by Sony Interactive Entertainment. Sony introduced the brand in 1994. It now consists of four types of home consoles, as well as a media center, an online service, a line of controllers, two handhelds, a phone, and multiple magazines.

[S]

Smart glasses are self-contained mixed-reality glasses. When they exist, they will look a lot like everyday eye glasses.

Snapchat Lenses are used to add real-time special effects and sounds to snaps based on geofilters.

Stereoscopy is a technique for creating or enhancing the illusion of depth in an image by means of stereopsis for binocular vision or surround sound.

[V]

Virtual reality (VR) is a computer technology that replicates an environment, real or imagined, and simulates a user's physical presence in a way that allows the user to interact with it. Virtual realities artificially create sensory experiences, which can include sight, touch, hearing and smell.

The Visual Web describes a collection of internet content searchable by images, not just by text.

[W]

Watson is IBM's question-answering computer built on AI. It is said to be the world's smartest machine.

[X]

Xbox is a video gaming brand created and owned by Microsoft. The brand also represents applications (games), streaming services, and an online service called Xbox Live.

[Z]

Zees a shortening of Generation Z.

Acknowledgements

There are many differences between self-publishers like us and traditional authors. The first, is that we have to assemble our own team of professionals to create, design and produce this book, and second, it takes a global village filled with resources, ideas and suggestions.

Let's start with the team we have assembled. It is comprised of a several old-hands and one notable new addition. He has been an extremely valuable member of our self-publishing team. Let's start there:

- **Josh Bernoff.** Our content editor, the author of four books himself, has kept us on track and set a high bar for accuracy along our path. He has forced us to curb the excessive enthusiasm so that we can provide a balanced view. Josh suggested the title that we are using. He also endured highly unreasonable deadlines and myriad changes that happen when you are trying to write an enduring book about a dynamic subject, such as we tend to choose. His contributions are many, and our gratitude is great.
- **Merlina McGovern.** Thanks to Merlina, who diligently and graciously pointed out the many errors and inconsistencies in our imperfect prose.

- **Paula Israel.** Through seven books, she has performed the dreaded "wife test" on books authored and co-authored by Shel Israel. She makes certain that jargon is purged and that the reader should not have to struggle to understand the points we endeavor to make. While we struggle to make our books useful, Paula endeavors to keep them interesting, and we owe her a significant debt.

- **Shawn Welch.** This is the third time Shawn has served as our internal designer and Amazon liaison. He knows so much about self-publishing that he could write a book on it. In fact, he did. He is co-author of *APE: Author, Publisher, Entrepreneur*, the unofficial guidebook to clueless authors, a bible that we keep handy when doing our books.

- **Nico Nicomedes.** As the cover designer for *Age of Context*, he was our obvious choice for designing this sequel cover. We wanted to continue the graphic spirit of our previous book. Nico is fun, fast and resourceful in providing authors who may not be able to express what they want with precisely what they, in fact, wanted.

- **Jeffrey Kafer.** We are happy to count on Jeffrey as our Audible voice for the third consecutive time. He is a professional audio narrator. As our business partner for Audible, he handles our audio books, which is the fastest growing segment of our book-selling business.

- **Karelyn Eve Lambert.** Our virtual assistant has served as our proofreader, utility infielder and order fulfillment coordinator for our past three books. She is the glue in our process.

This is a team to which we owe a great deal. If you ever decide to take the self-publishing route, we will be glad to connect you with each of them, except for Paula Israel, with whom we have an exclusive relationship.

That brings us to our global village. In 2005, we became the first authors ever to publish early versions of our entire book, *Naked Conversations*, in our blogs. Since then we have remained prolific in what we post in social media, particularly Facebook, where we regularly hang out.

We do this for multiple reasons. First, our Facebook friends have been a valuable source of ideas, contacts, corrections and advice. They can be savage at times, but they are always constructive. It is far better to be told our cover is ugly on a Facebook page than to be clueless as to why people aren't buying the book.

In the year that we posted excerpts, lead requests, draft chapters and requests for advice, more than a thousand people have left comments. Many of them influenced what we wrote—or rewrote.

We thank each and every one of them. Your conversation has helped to guide us.

In this village there are those who gave us specific ideas and leads for content that appears in this book. We would like to spotlight each of these people. Special thanks to:

- Laurent Haug
- Jeris Jc Miller
- Shel Holtz
- Rob Mowery
- Brian Hayashi
- Michael Markman
- Brett King
- Peter Dawson
- Julien Blin
- Yeva Roberts
- Gene Deel
- Jason Thibeault
- Christopher Penn
- Scott Monty
- Richard Binhammer
- Kelly Thresher

- Daniel Marchand
- Jeremy Wright
- Offir Gutelzon
- Ken Siegmann
- Will Pate
- Viv Craske
- Mojtaba Tabatabaie
- Mark Stahlman
- Lionel Menchaca Jr.
- Shannon John Clark
- Sandy Adam
- Nina Stephanie
- Isaac Pigott
- Dennis Yu
- Dagan Henderson
- Jim Minatel
- Roger McNamee
- Deirdre Porter
- Irena Cronin
- Marc Canter
- Danette Jaeb

If we somehow overlooked you, please notify ShelIsrael1@gmail.com, and we will add you to a future edition.

+++++

Index